GRAPHIC EXPEDITIONS

Egypt's Mysterious PYRAMIDS

AN *Isabel Soto* ARCHAEOLOGY ADVENTURE

by Agnieszka Biskup
illustrated by Roger Stewart

Consultant:
Laurel Bestock
Assistant Professor of Egyptology and Archaeology
Brown University
Providence, Rhode Island

CAPSTONE PRESS
a capstone imprint

Graphic Library is published by Capstone Press,
1710 Roe Crest Drive, North Mankato, Minnesota 56003.
www.capstonepub.com

Printed in the United States of America in Stevens Point, Wisconsin.
032012
006625R

Books published by Capstone Press are manufactured with paper containing at least 10 percent post-consumer waste.

Library of Congress Cataloging-in-Publication Data
Biskup, Agnieszka.
Egypt's mysterious pyramids : an Isabel Soto archaeology adventure / by Agnieszka Biskup; illustrated by Roger Stewart.
p. cm.—(Graphic library. Graphic expeditions)
Summary: "In graphic novel format, follows the adventures of Isabel Soto as she discovers the secrets about Egypt's great pyramids"—Provided by publisher.
Includes bibliographical references and index.
ISBN 978-1-4296-7544-4 (library binding)
ISBN 978-1-4296-7992-3 (paperback)
1. Pyramids—Egypt—Comic books, strips, etc. 2. Pyramids—Egypt—Juvenile literature. 3. Egypt—Antiquities—Comic books, strips, etc. 4. Graphic novels. I. Stewart, Roger. II. Title. III. Series: Graphic library. Graphic expeditions.
DT63.B54 2012
932—dc23 2011028643

Designer
Alison Thiele

Editor
Aaron Sautter

Production Specialist
Laura Manthe

Photo credits: Shutterstock: Pius Lee, 9

Design elements: Shutterstock/Chen Ping Hung (framed edge design); mmmm (world map design); Mushakesa (abstract lines design); Najin (old parchment design)

TABLE OF CONTENTS

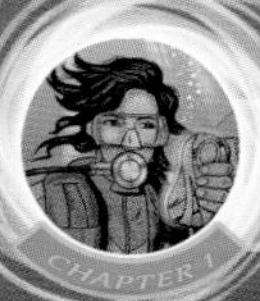
CHAPTER 1

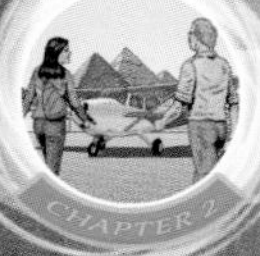
CHAPTER 2

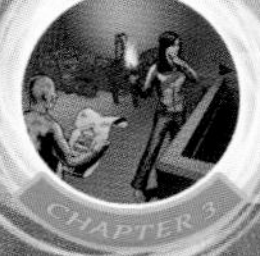
CHAPTER 3

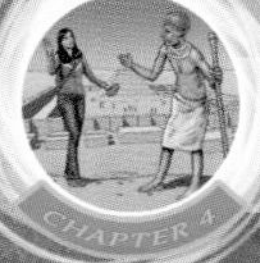
CHAPTER 4

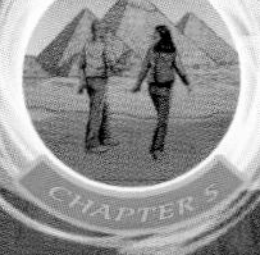
CHAPTER 5

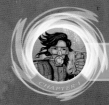

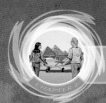

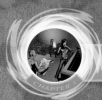

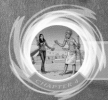

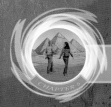

CHAPTER 1 SUNKEN WONDER

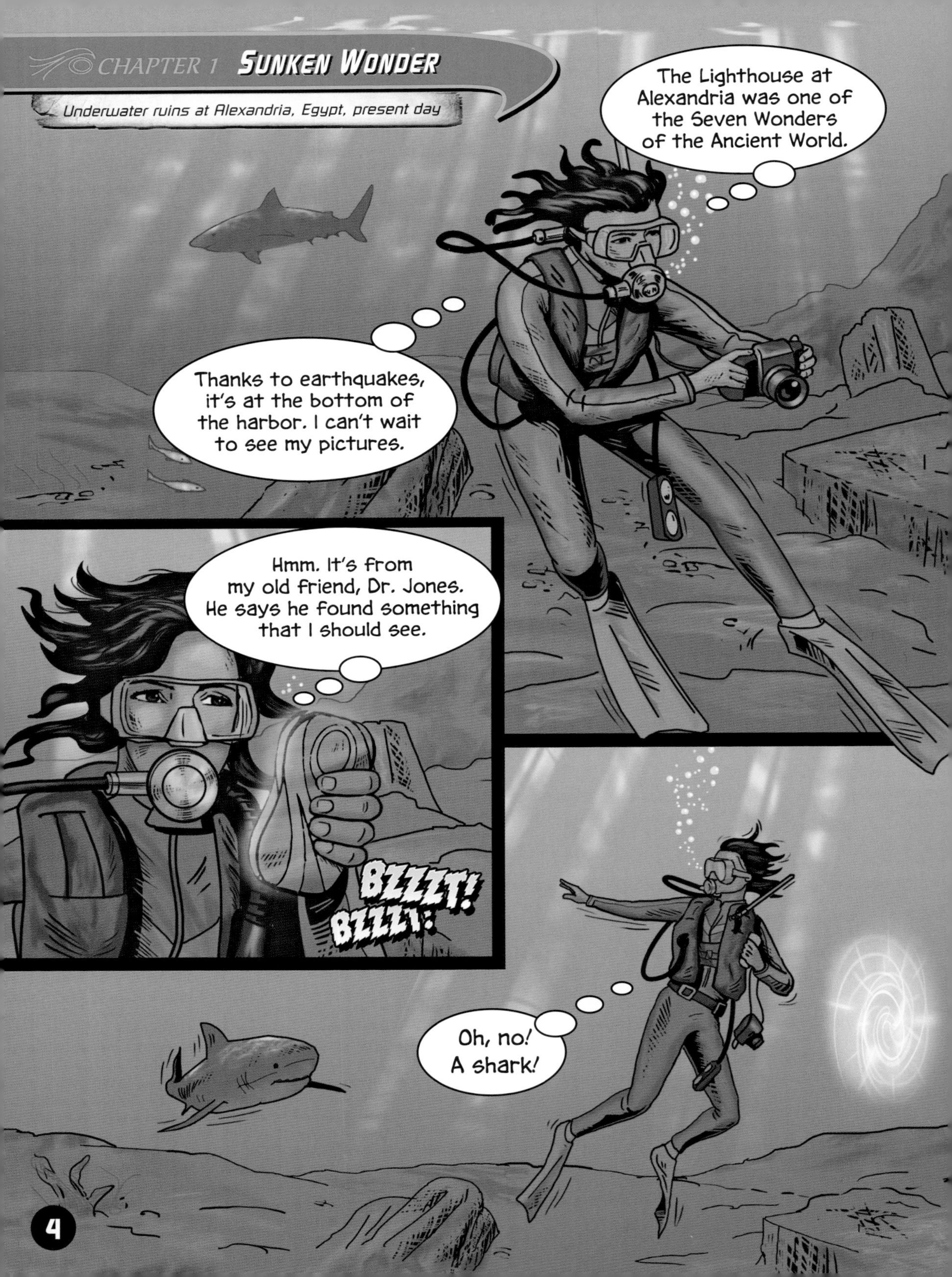
Underwater ruins at Alexandria, Egypt, present day
The Lighthouse at Alexandria was one of the Seven Wonders of the Ancient World.
Thanks to earthquakes, it's at the bottom of the harbor. I can't wait to see my pictures.
Hmm. It's from my old friend, Dr. Jones. He says he found something that I should see.
BZZZT! BZZZT!
Oh, no! A shark!

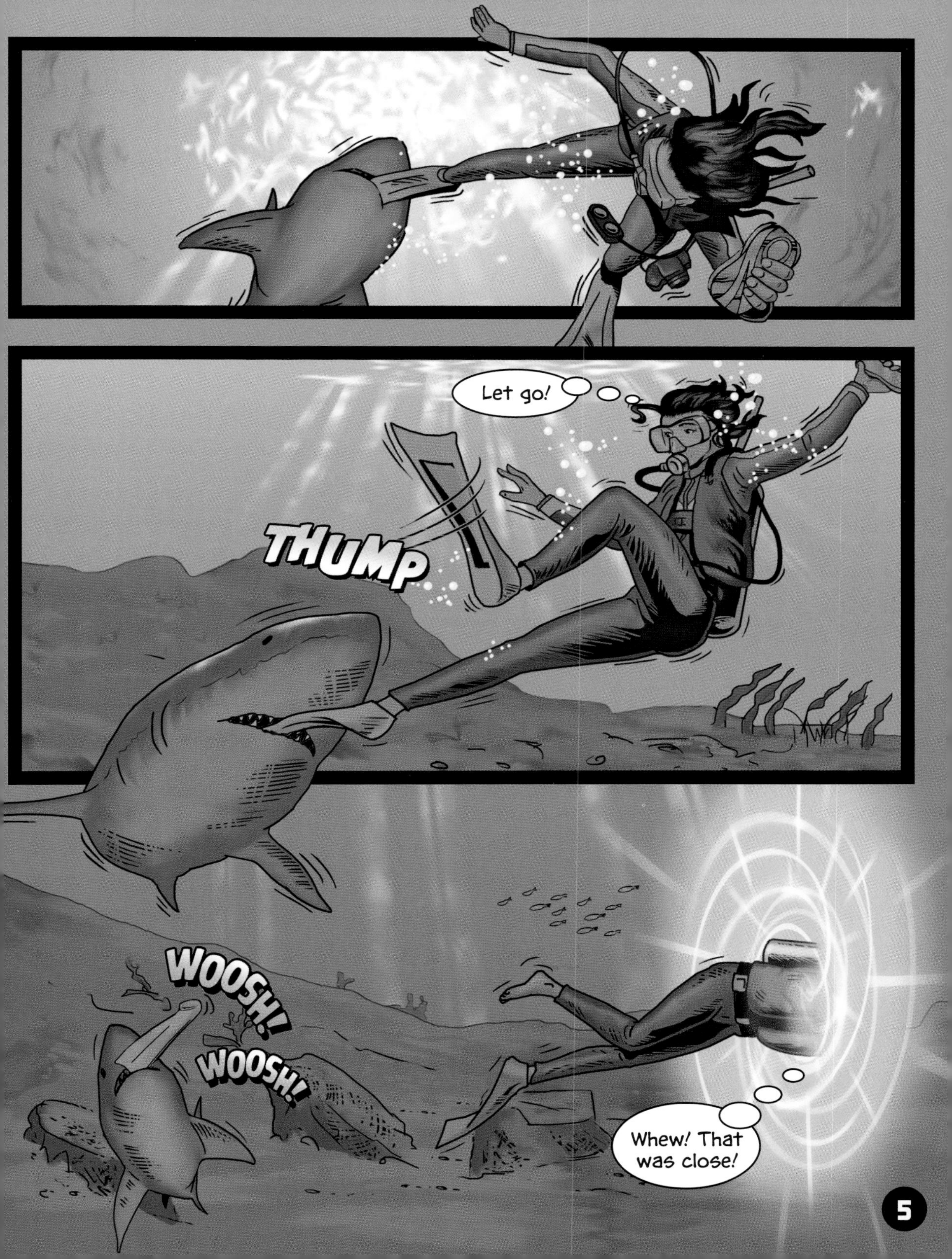
Let go!
THUMP
WOOSH!
WOOSH!
Whew! That was close!

CHAPTER 2 THE PYRAMIDS OF GIZA

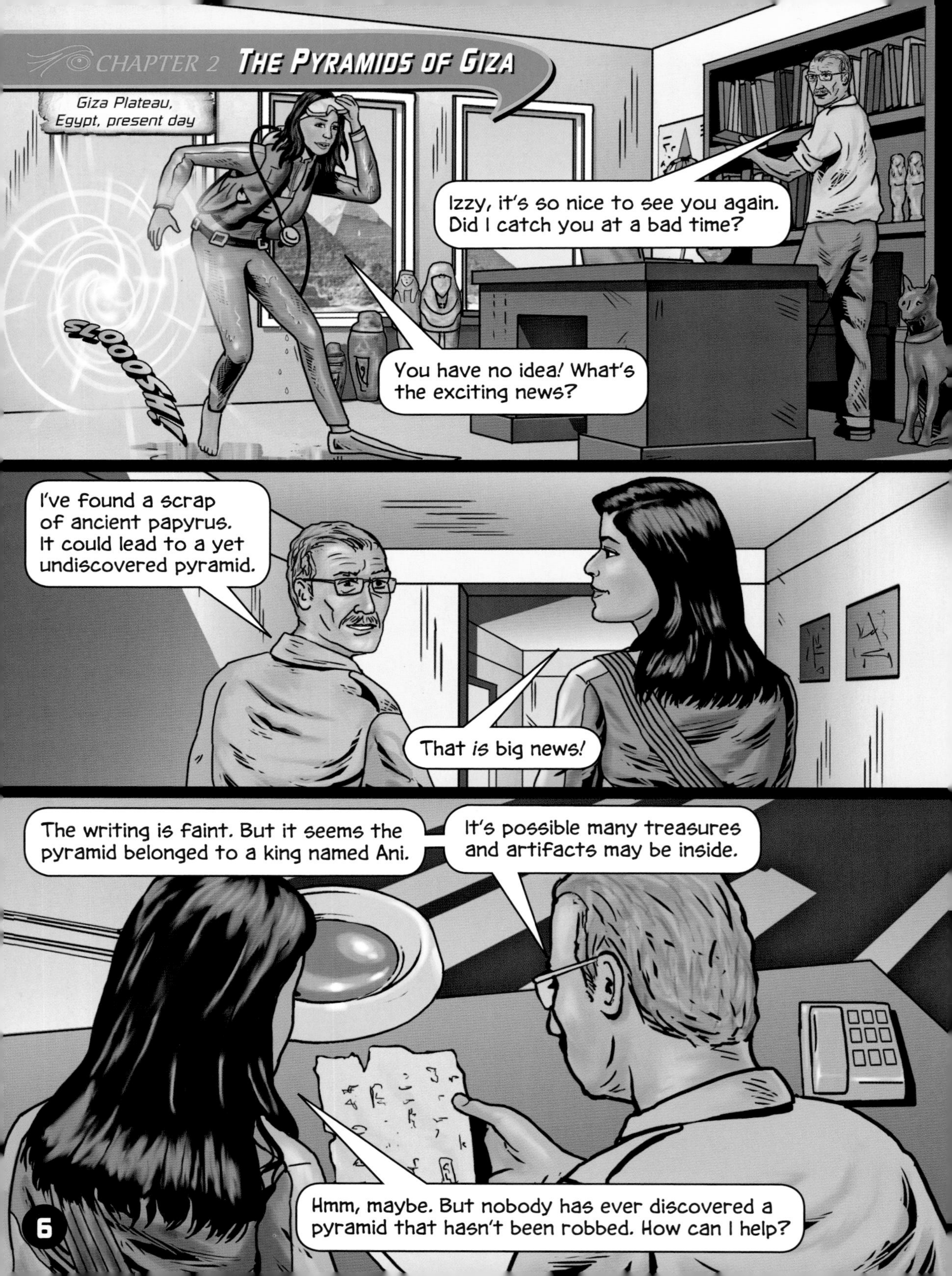
Giza Plateau,
Egypt, present day
SLOOSH!
Izzy, it's so nice to see you again. Did I catch you at a bad time?
You have no idea! What's the exciting news?
I've found a scrap of ancient papyrus. It could lead to a yet undiscovered pyramid.
That *is* big news!
The writing is faint. But it seems the pyramid belonged to a king named Ani.
It's possible many treasures and artifacts may be inside.
Hmm, maybe. But nobody has ever discovered a pyramid that hasn't been robbed. How can I help?

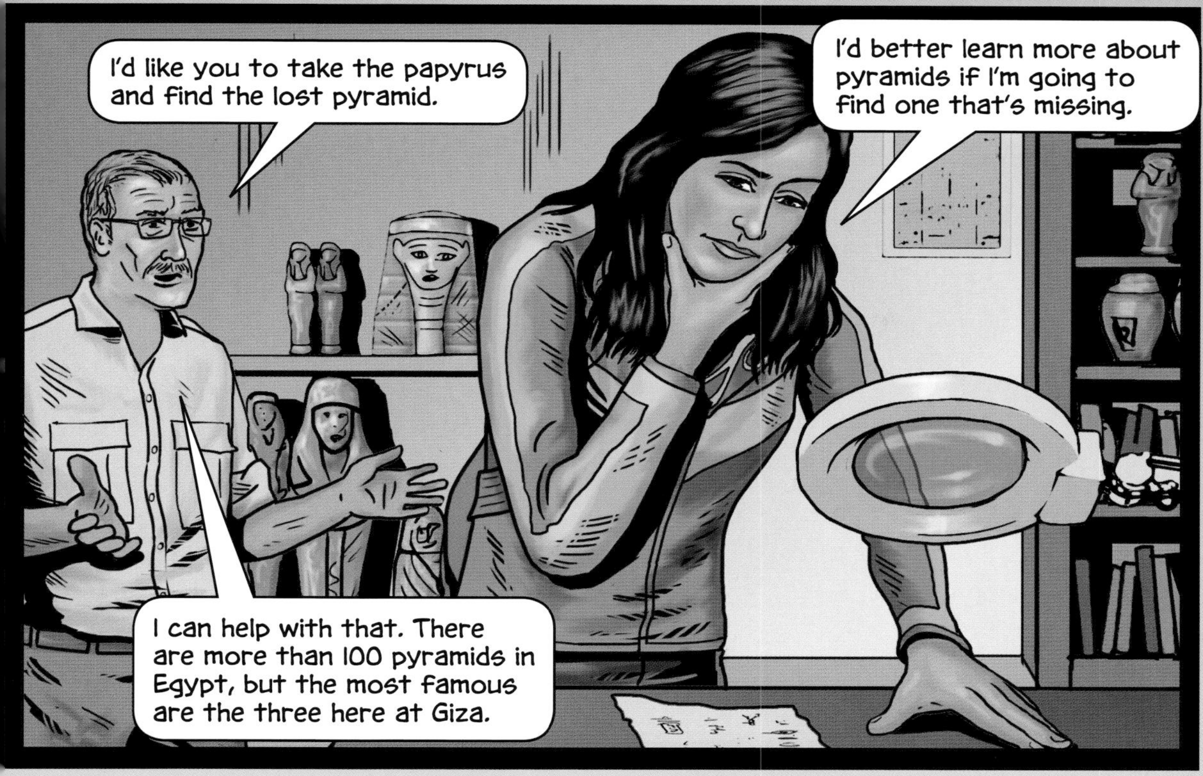
I'd like you to take the papyrus and find the lost pyramid.
I'd better learn more about pyramids if I'm going to find one that's missing.
I can help with that. There are more than 100 pyramids in Egypt, but the most famous are the three here at Giza.

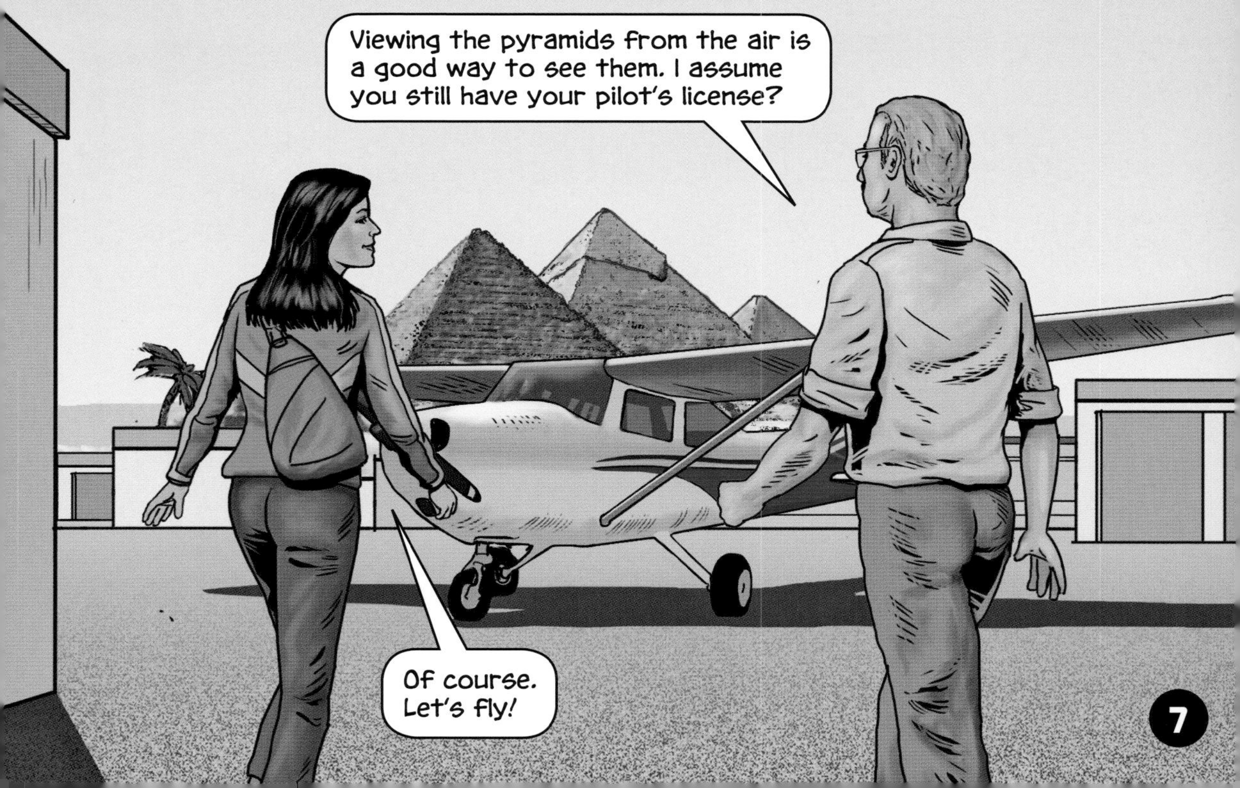
Viewing the pyramids from the air is a good way to see them. I assume you still have your pilot's license?
Of course. Let's fly!

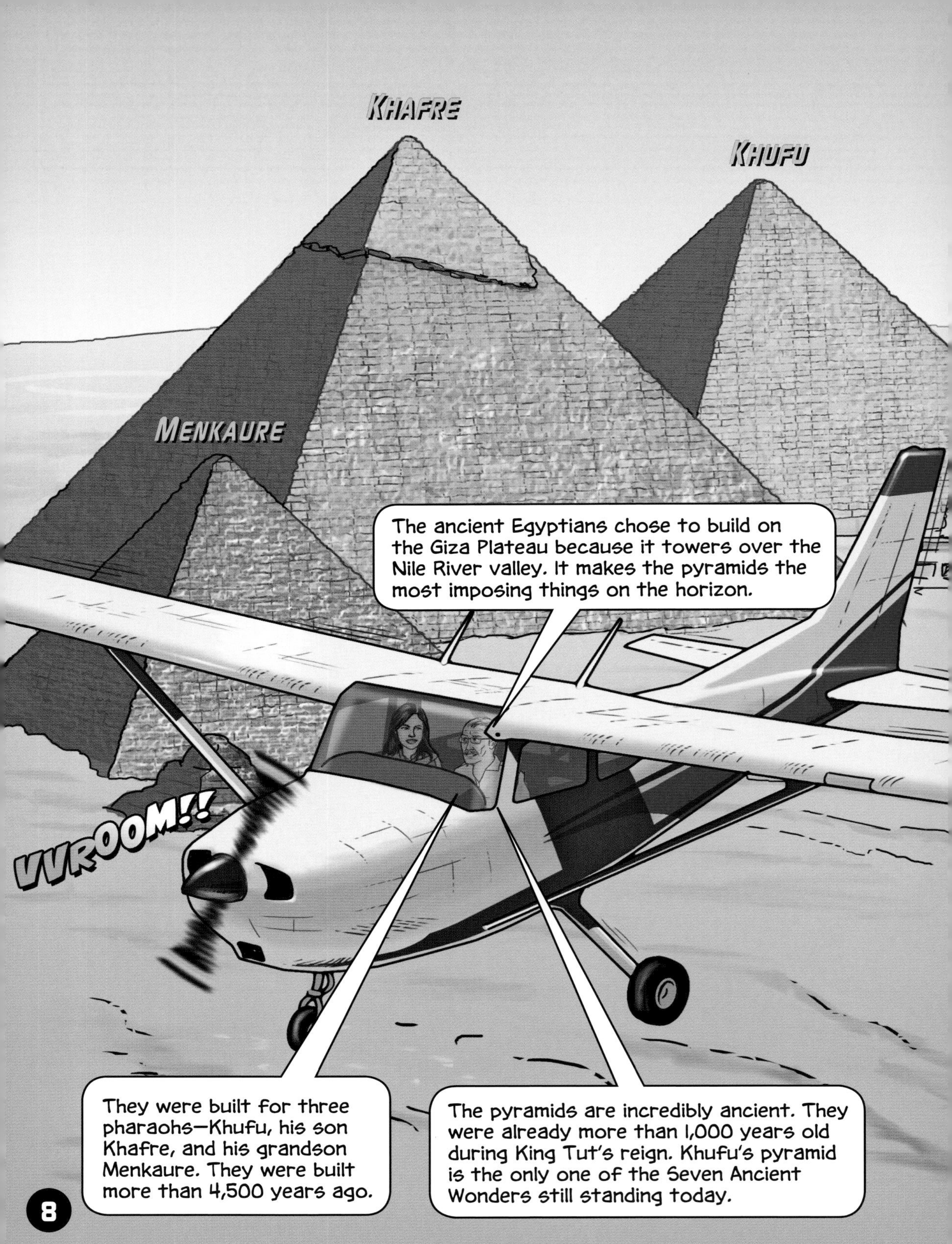

KHAFRE
KHUFU
MENKAURE
The ancient Egyptians chose to build on the Giza Plateau because it towers over the Nile River valley. It makes the pyramids the most imposing things on the horizon.
VVROOM!!
They were built for three pharaohs—Khufu, his son Khafre, and his grandson Menkaure. They were built more than 4,500 years ago.
The pyramids are incredibly ancient. They were already more than 1,000 years old during King Tut's reign. Khufu's pyramid is the only one of the Seven Ancient Wonders still standing today.

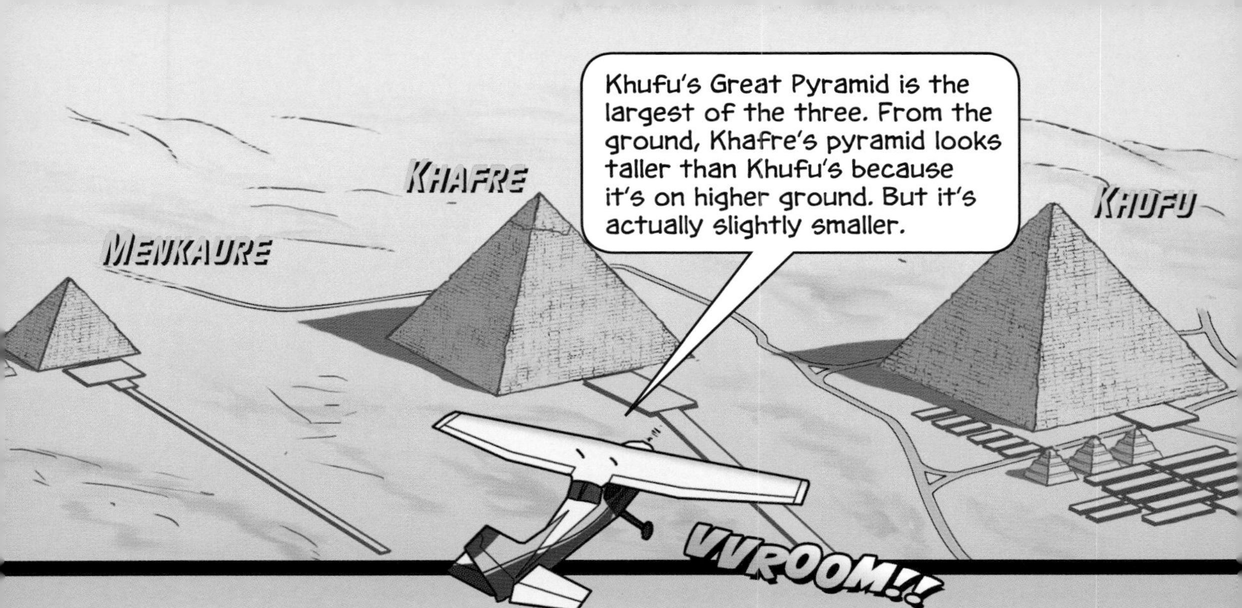
Khufu's Great Pyramid is the largest of the three. From the ground, Khafre's pyramid looks taller than Khufu's because it's on higher ground. But it's actually slightly smaller.
MENKAURE
KHAFRE
KHUFU
VVROOM!!

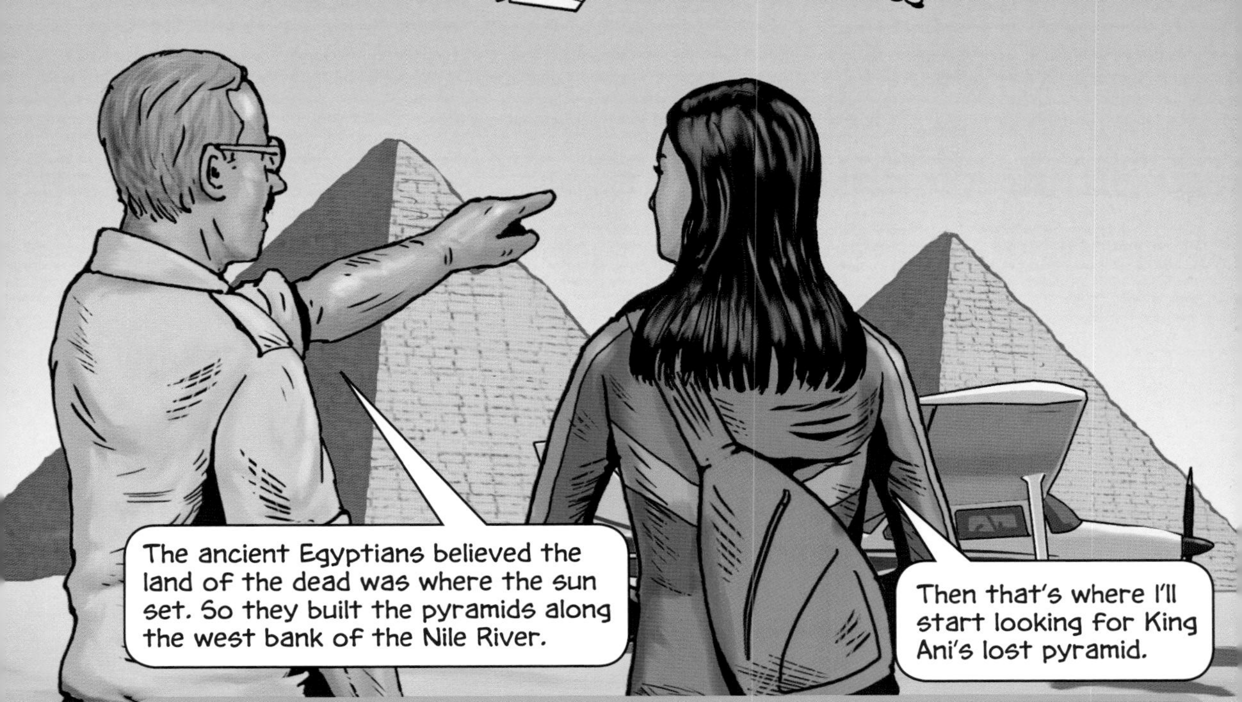
The ancient Egyptians believed the land of the dead was where the sun set. So they built the pyramids along the west bank of the Nile River.
Then that's where I'll start looking for King Ani's lost pyramid.

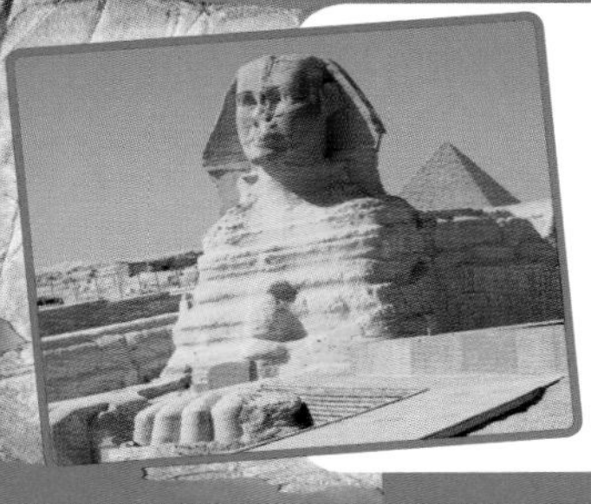

THE SPHINX

The Great Sphinx sits near the pyramids of Giza. It has the body of a lion and a human head. It is believed the sphinx symbolized the Egyptian sun god Ra. The Great Sphinx was covered in sand up to its neck for hundreds of years. Some people think the face on the Sphinx may be of the pharaoh Khafre.

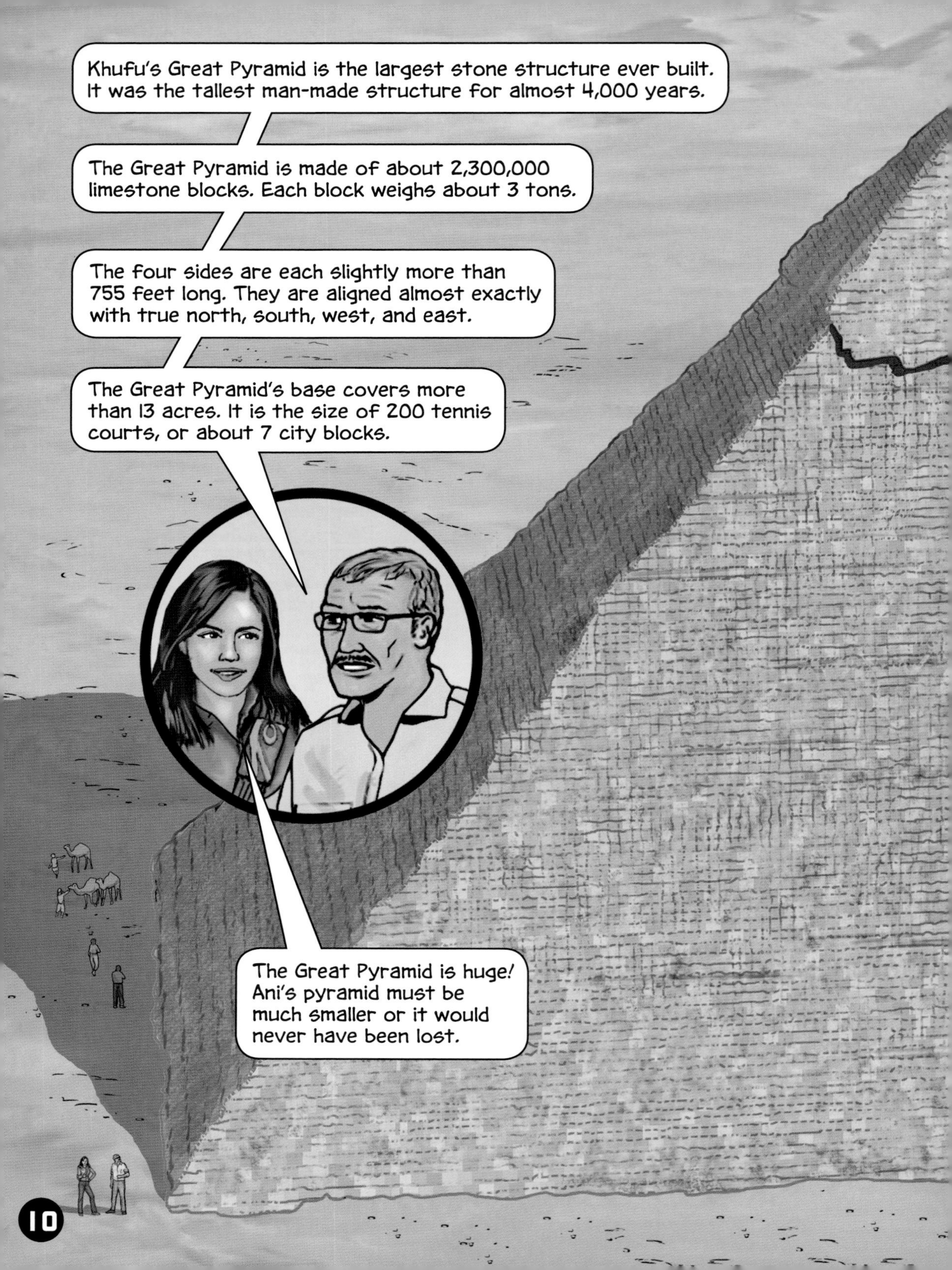
Khufu's Great Pyramid is the largest stone structure ever built. It was the tallest man-made structure for almost 4,000 years.
The Great Pyramid is made of about 2,300,000 limestone blocks. Each block weighs about 3 tons.
The four sides are each slightly more than 755 feet long. They are aligned almost exactly with true north, south, west, and east.
The Great Pyramid's base covers more than 13 acres. It is the size of 200 tennis courts, or about 7 city blocks.
The Great Pyramid is huge! Ani's pyramid must be much smaller or it would never have been lost.

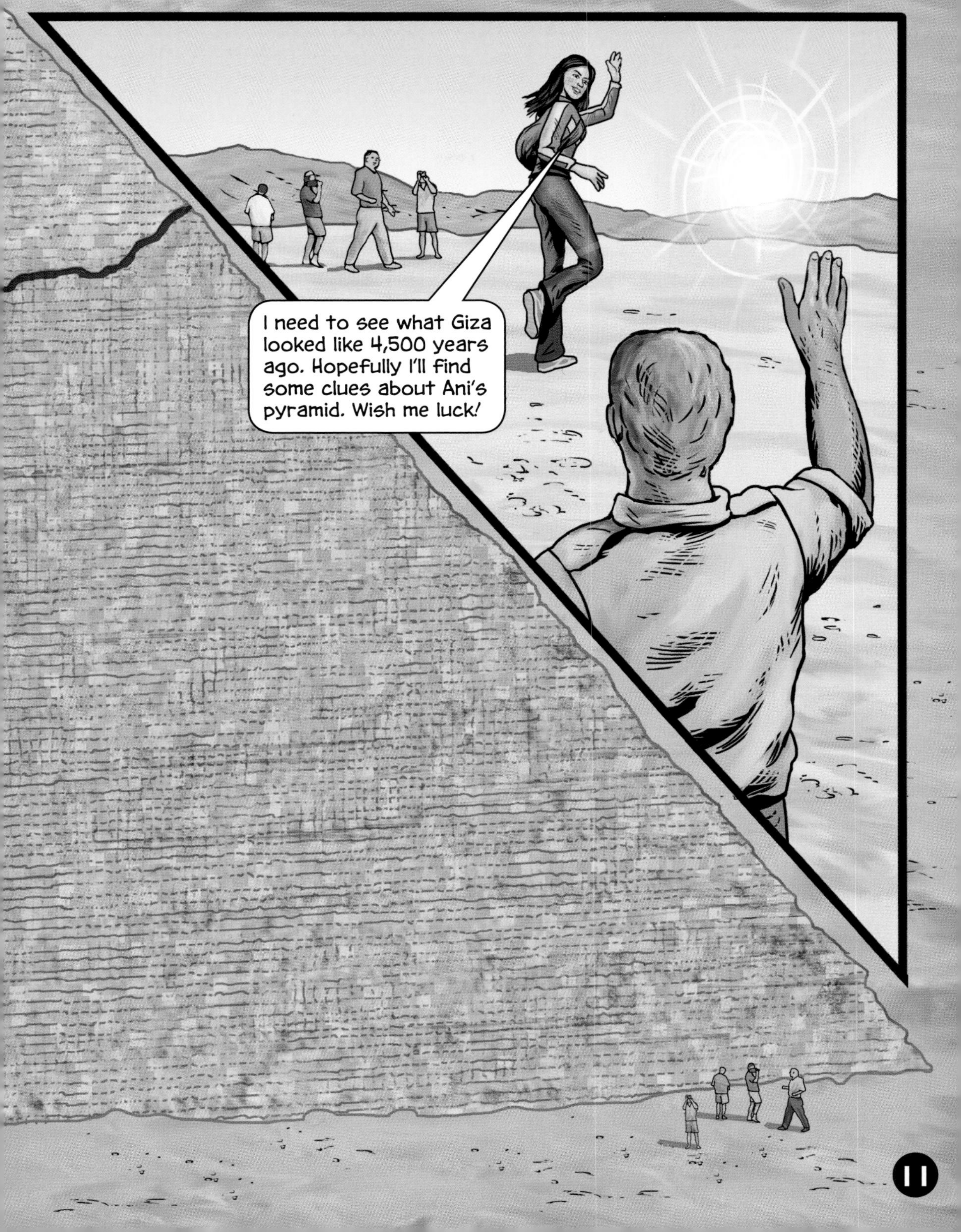
I need to see what Giza looked like 4,500 years ago. Hopefully I'll find some clues about Ani's pyramid. Wish me luck!

CHAPTER 3 Secrets of the Pyramids

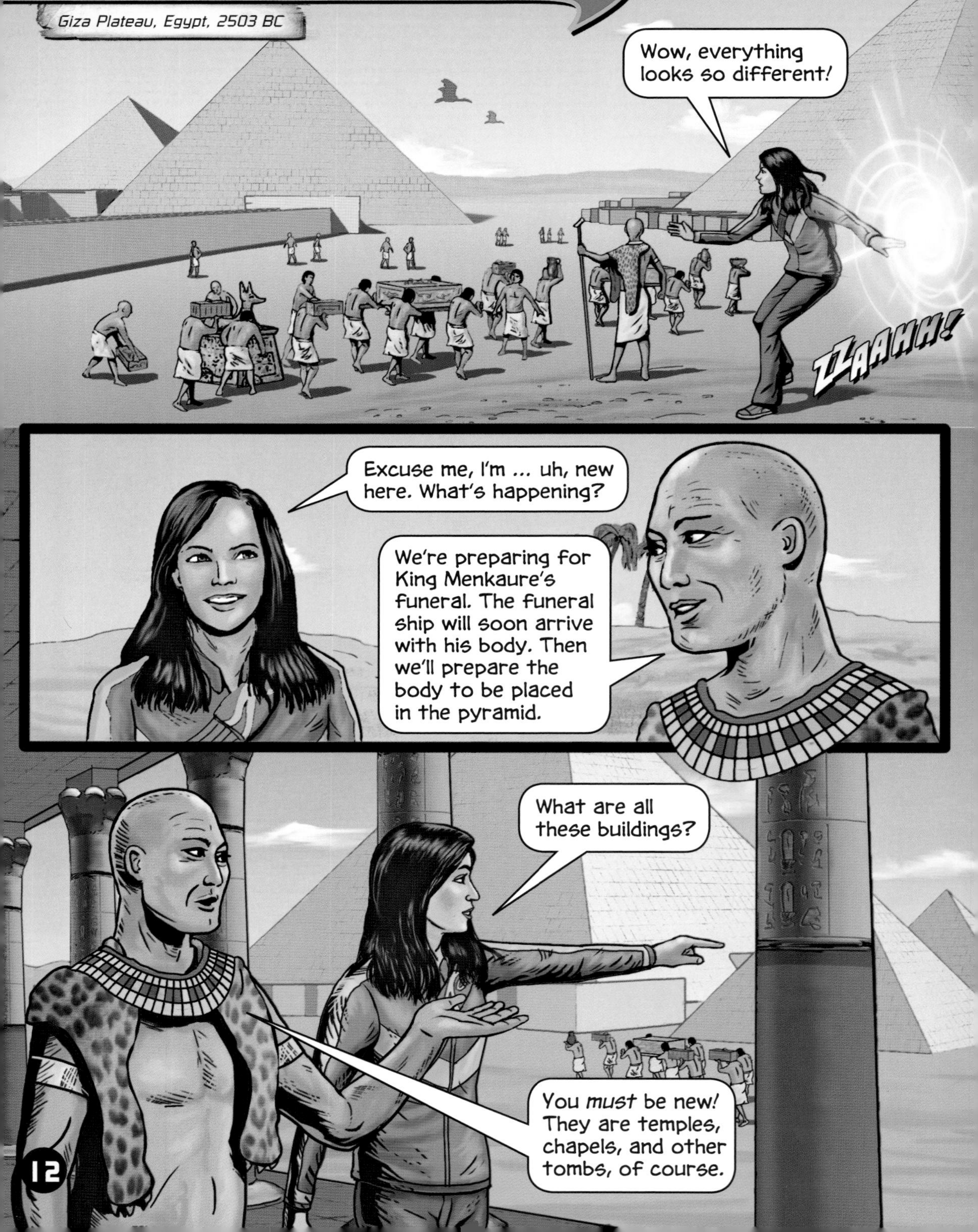
Giza Plateau, Egypt, 2503 BC
Wow, everything looks so different!
ZZAAHH!
Excuse me, I'm ... uh, new here. What's happening?
We're preparing for King Menkaure's funeral. The funeral ship will soon arrive with his body. Then we'll prepare the body to be placed in the pyramid.
What are all these buildings?
You *must* be new! They are temples, chapels, and other tombs, of course.

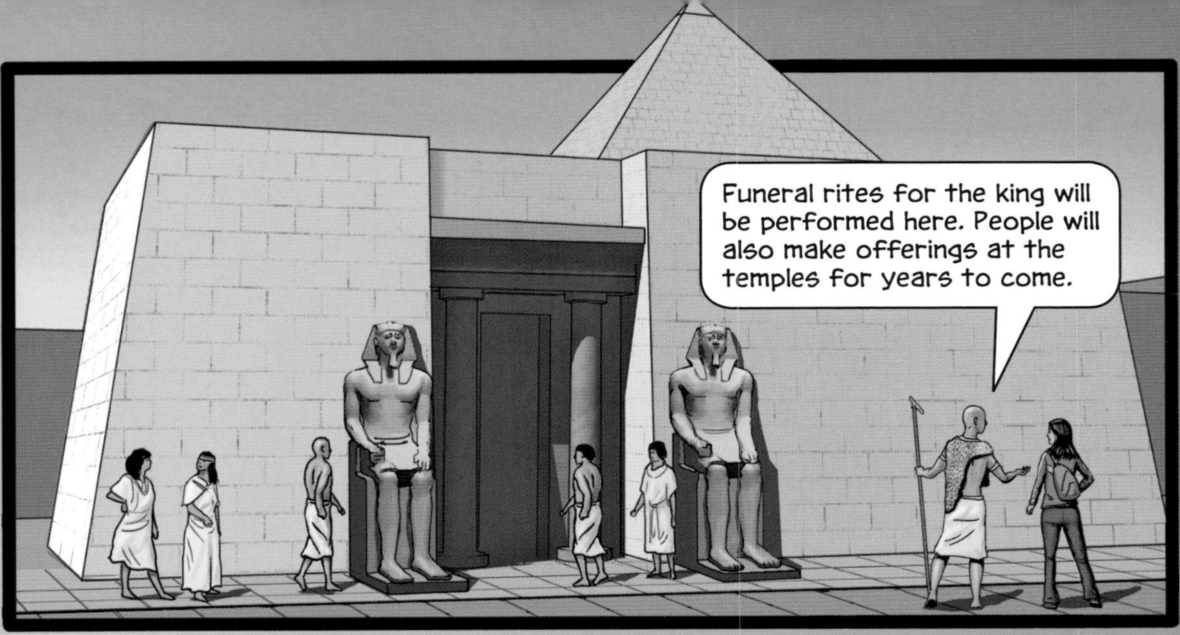
Funeral rites for the king will be performed here. People will also make offerings at the temples for years to come.

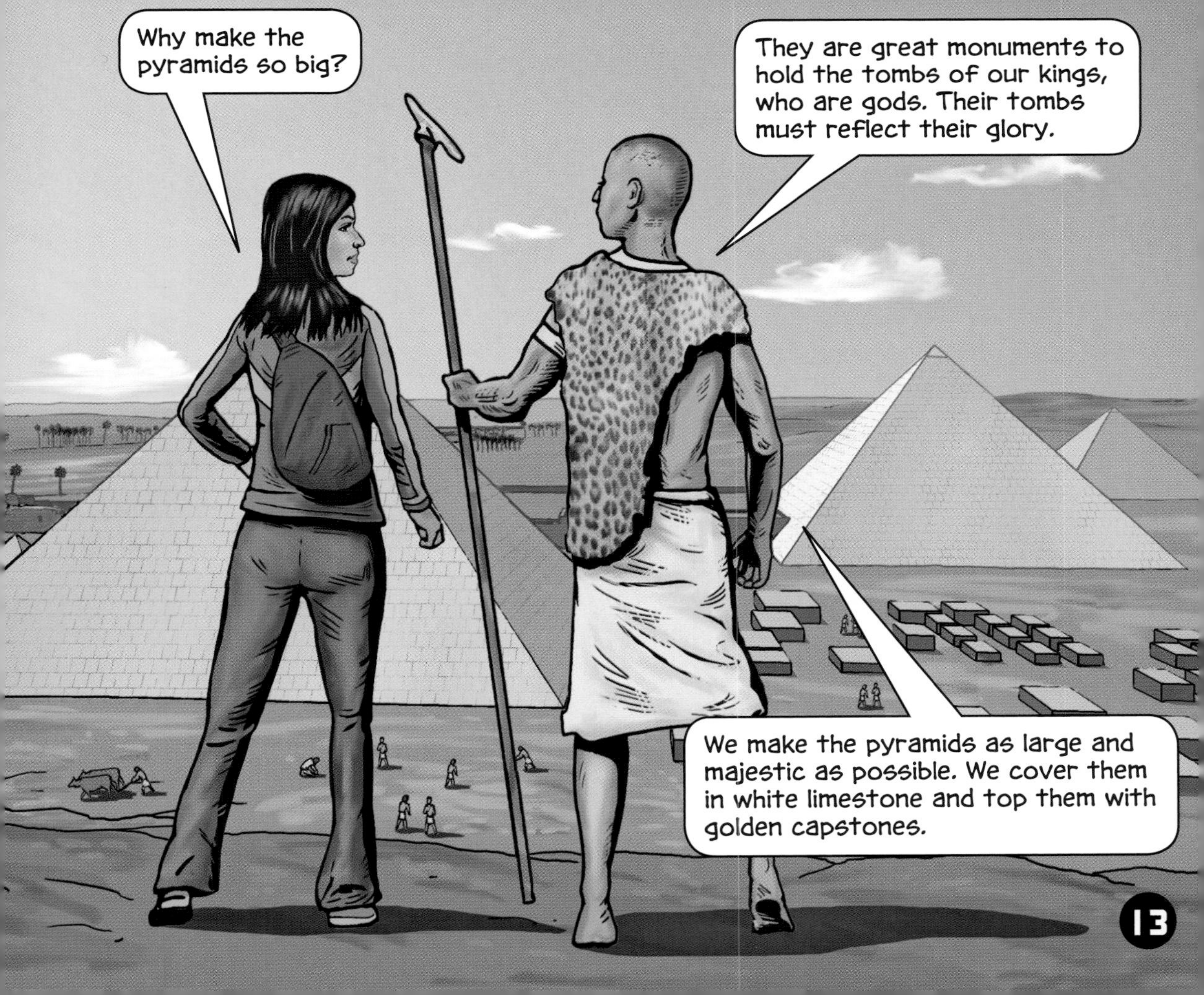
Why make the pyramids so big?
They are great monuments to hold the tombs of our kings, who are gods. Their tombs must reflect their glory.
We make the pyramids as large and majestic as possible. We cover them in white limestone and top them with golden capstones.

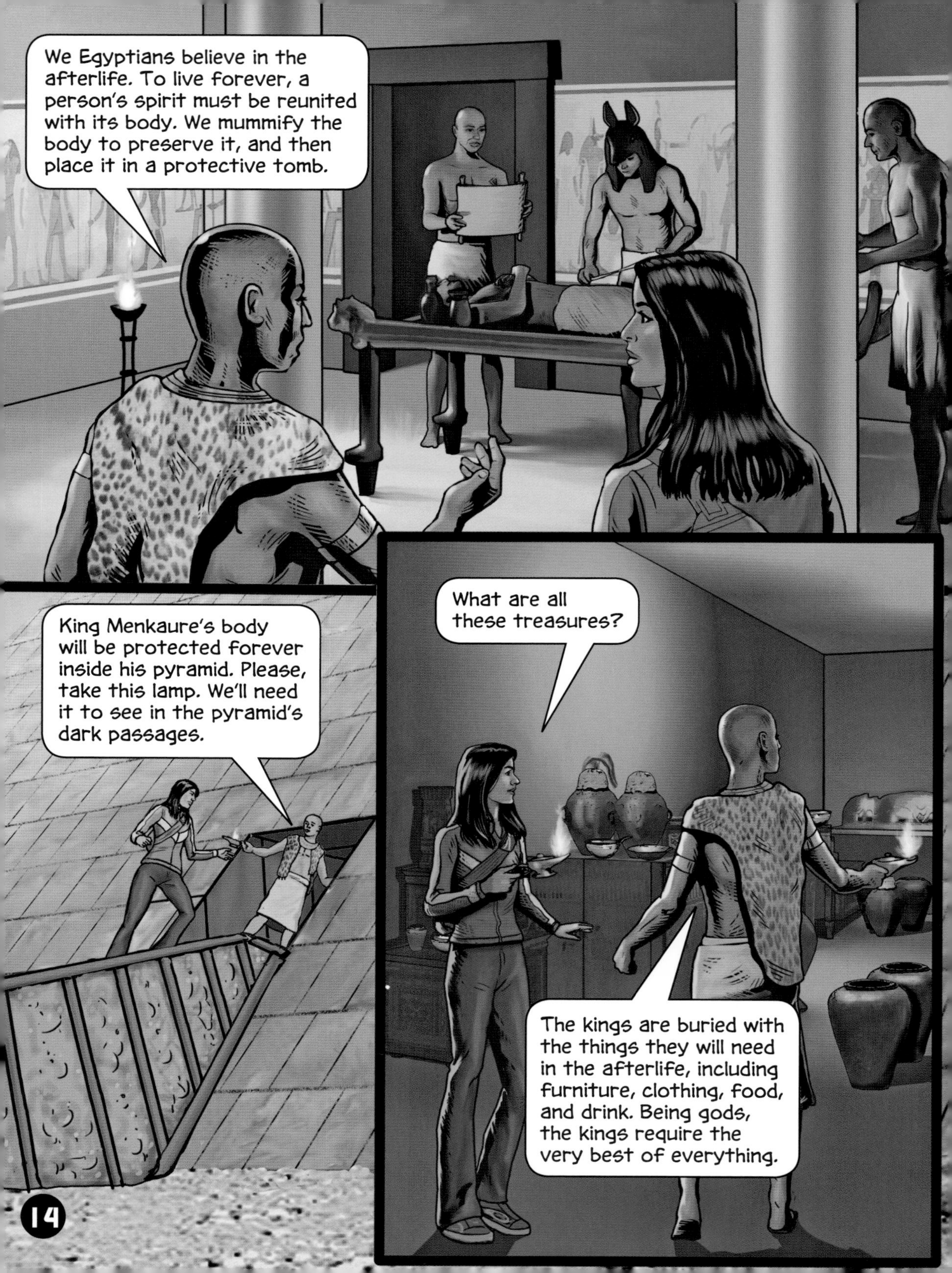
We Egyptians believe in the afterlife. To live forever, a person's spirit must be reunited with its body. We mummify the body to preserve it, and then place it in a protective tomb.
King Menkaure's body will be protected forever inside his pyramid. Please, take this lamp. We'll need it to see in the pyramid's dark passages.
What are all these treasures?
The kings are buried with the things they will need in the afterlife, including furniture, clothing, food, and drink. Being gods, the kings require the very best of everything.

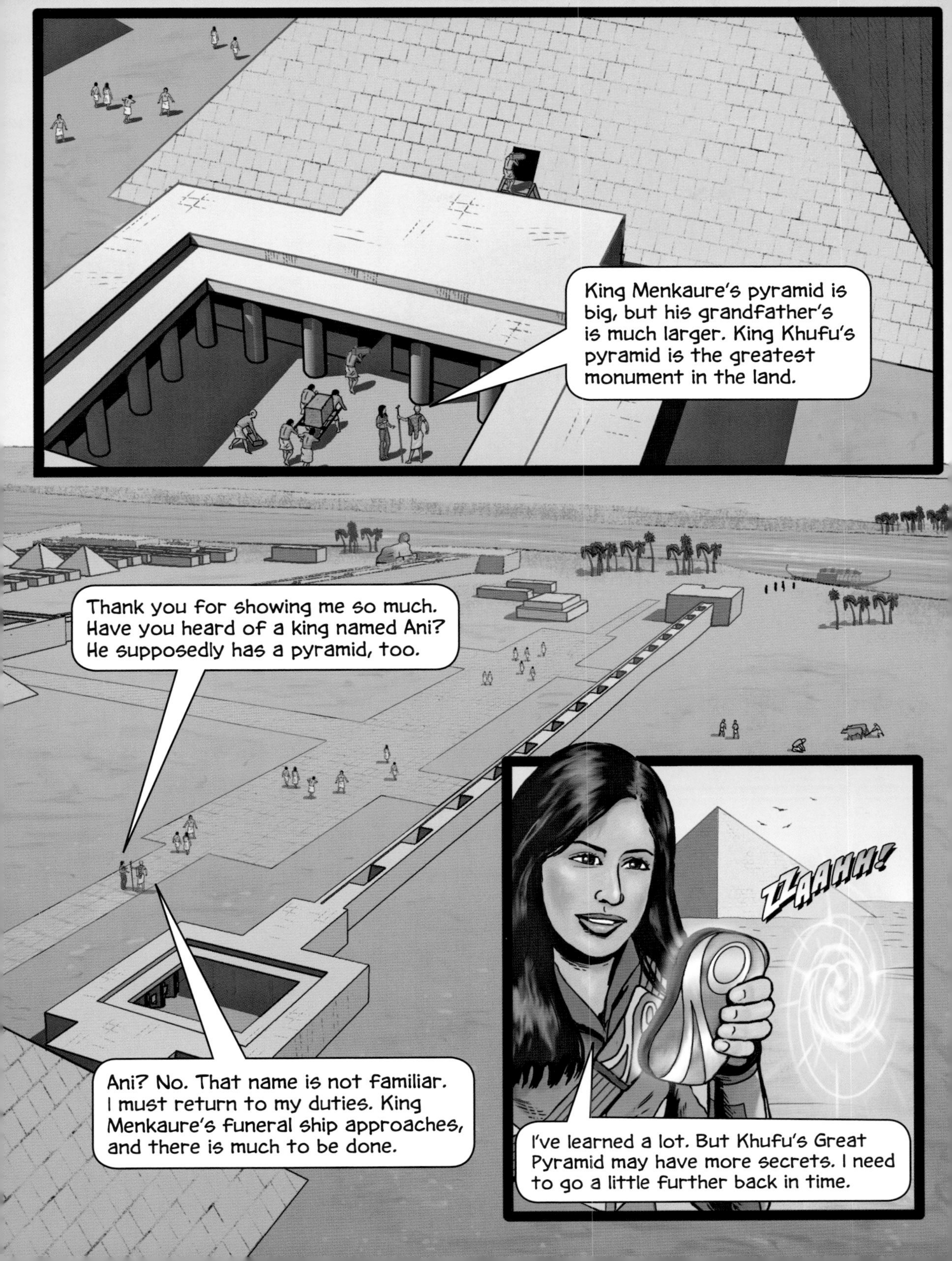
King Menkaure's pyramid is big, but his grandfather's is much larger. King Khufu's pyramid is the greatest monument in the land.
Thank you for showing me so much. Have you heard of a king named Ani? He supposedly has a pyramid, too.
Ani? No. That name is not familiar. I must return to my duties. King Menkaure's funeral ship approaches, and there is much to be done.
ZZAAHH!
I've learned a lot. But Khufu's Great Pyramid may have more secrets. I need to go a little further back in time.

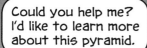

Could you help me? I'd like to learn more about this pyramid.

You're in luck, I'm Hemiunu, King Khufu's chief architect. Let me take you on a tour inside.

ZWOOSH!

This is the way to the King's Chamber. Follow me.

This is the Grand Gallery. The tomb isn't far now.

This is a relief after that cramped corridor. The ceiling here looks almost 30 feet high.

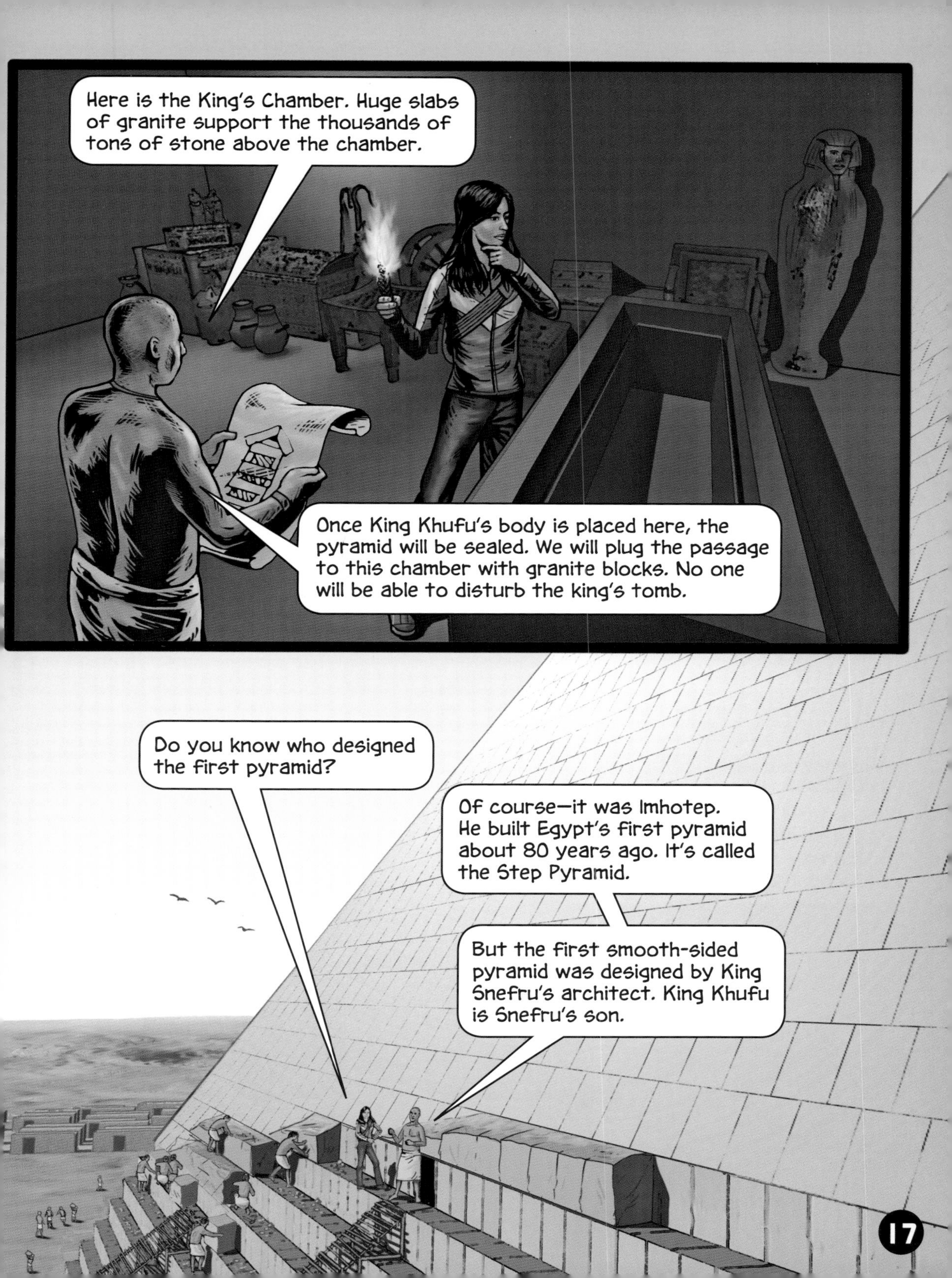
Here is the King's Chamber. Huge slabs of granite support the thousands of tons of stone above the chamber.
Once King Khufu's body is placed here, the pyramid will be sealed. We will plug the passage to this chamber with granite blocks. No one will be able to disturb the king's tomb.
Do you know who designed the first pyramid?
Of course—it was Imhotep. He built Egypt's first pyramid about 80 years ago. It's called the Step Pyramid.
But the first smooth-sided pyramid was designed by King Snefru's architect. King Khufu is Snefru's son.

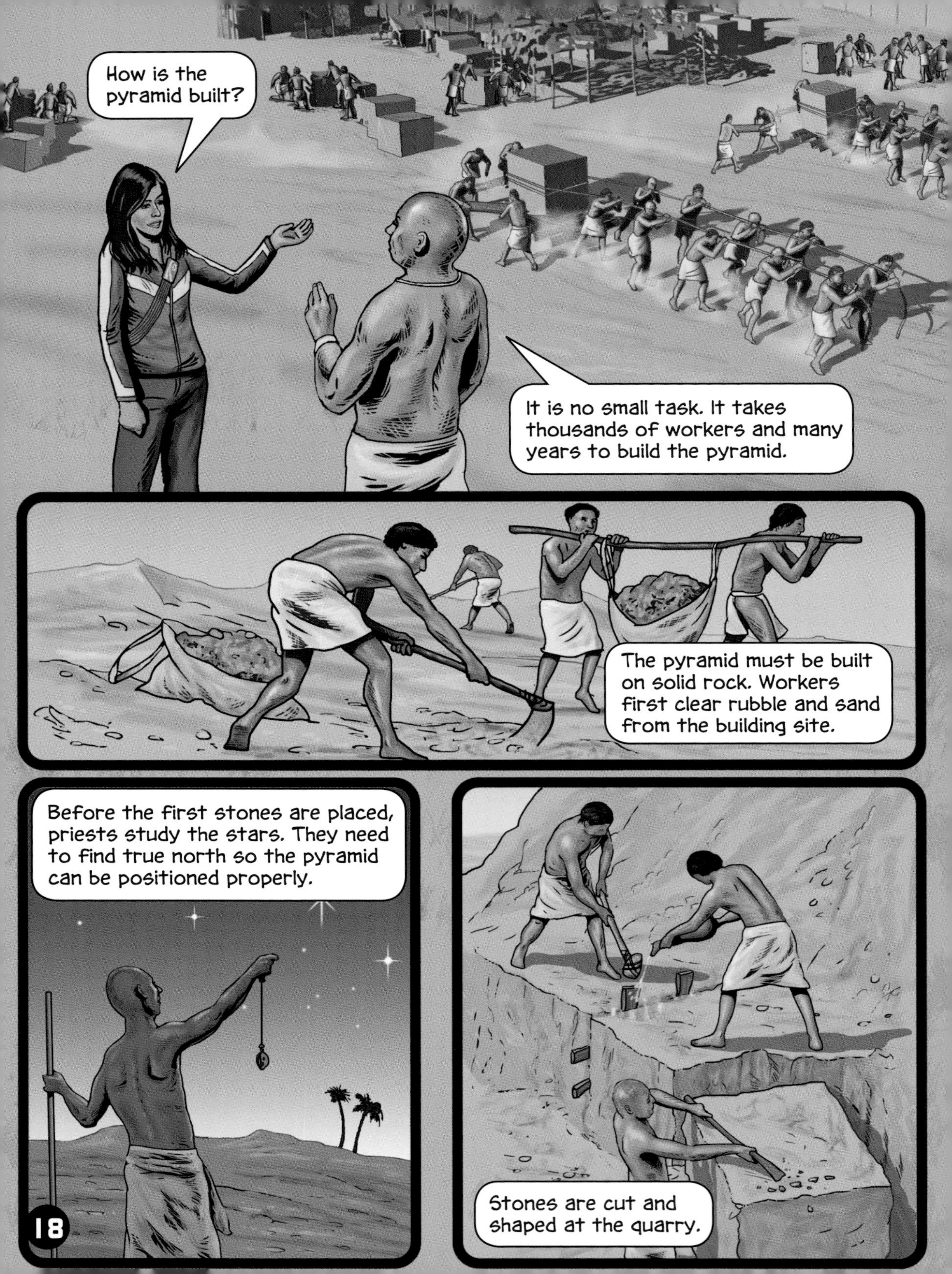
How is the pyramid built?
It is no small task. It takes thousands of workers and many years to build the pyramid.
The pyramid must be built on solid rock. Workers first clear rubble and sand from the building site.
Before the first stones are placed, priests study the stars. They need to find true north so the pyramid can be positioned properly.
Stones are cut and shaped at the quarry.

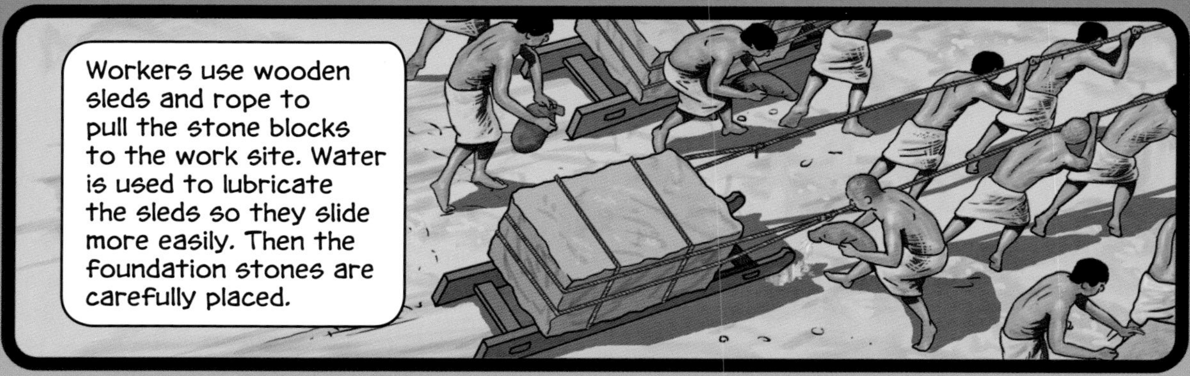
Workers use wooden sleds and rope to pull the stone blocks to the work site. Water is used to lubricate the sleds so they slide more easily. Then the foundation stones are carefully placed.

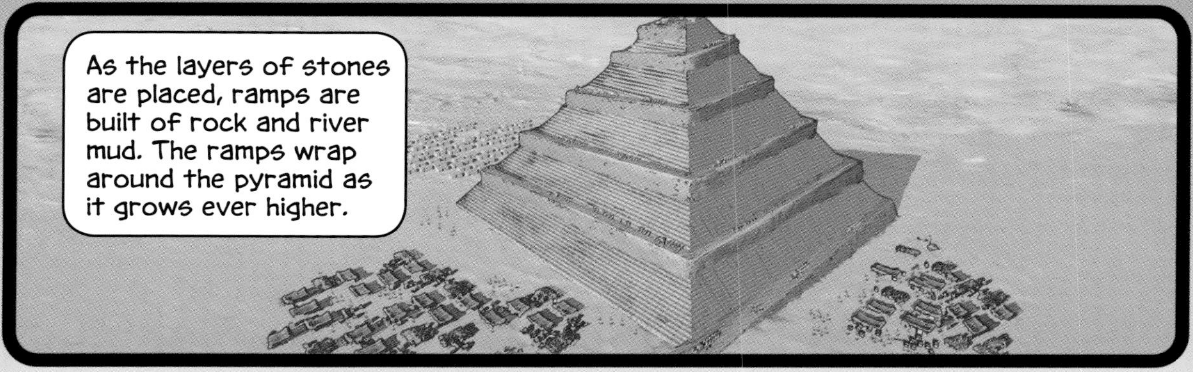
As the layers of stones are placed, ramps are built of rock and river mud. The ramps wrap around the pyramid as it grows ever higher.

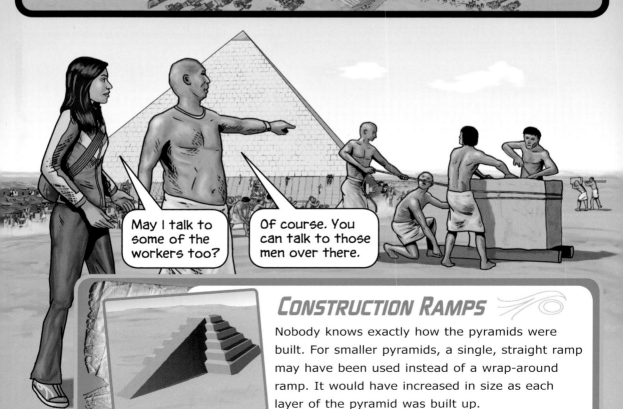

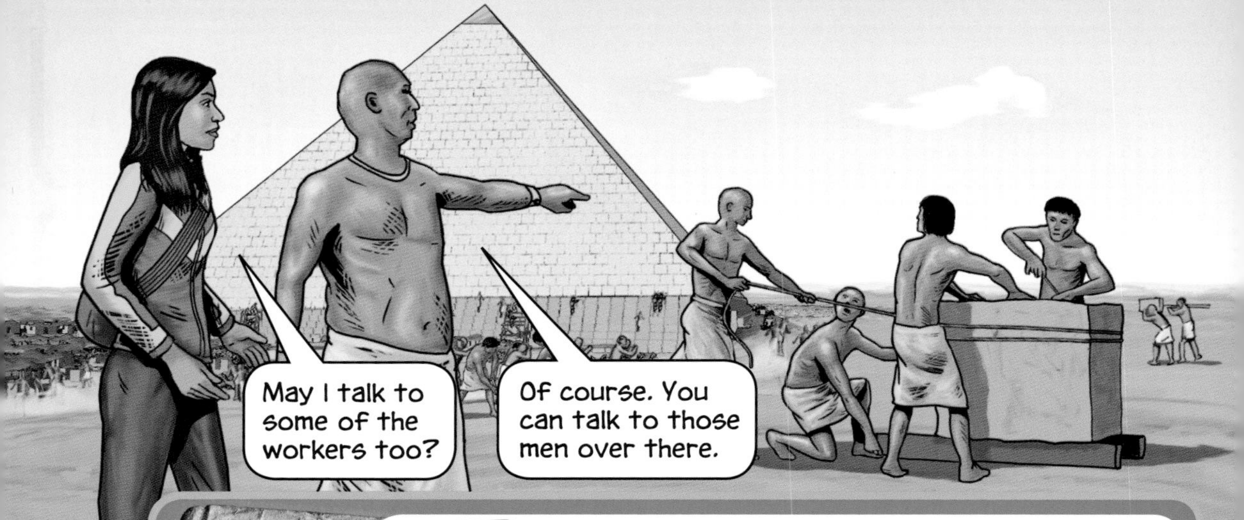
May I talk to some of the workers too?
Of course. You can talk to those men over there.

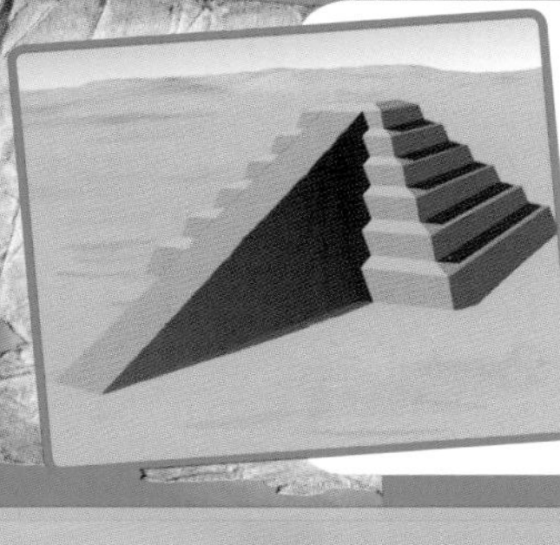

CONSTRUCTION RAMPS

Nobody knows exactly how the pyramids were built. For smaller pyramids, a single, straight ramp may have been used instead of a wrap-around ramp. It would have increased in size as each layer of the pyramid was built up.

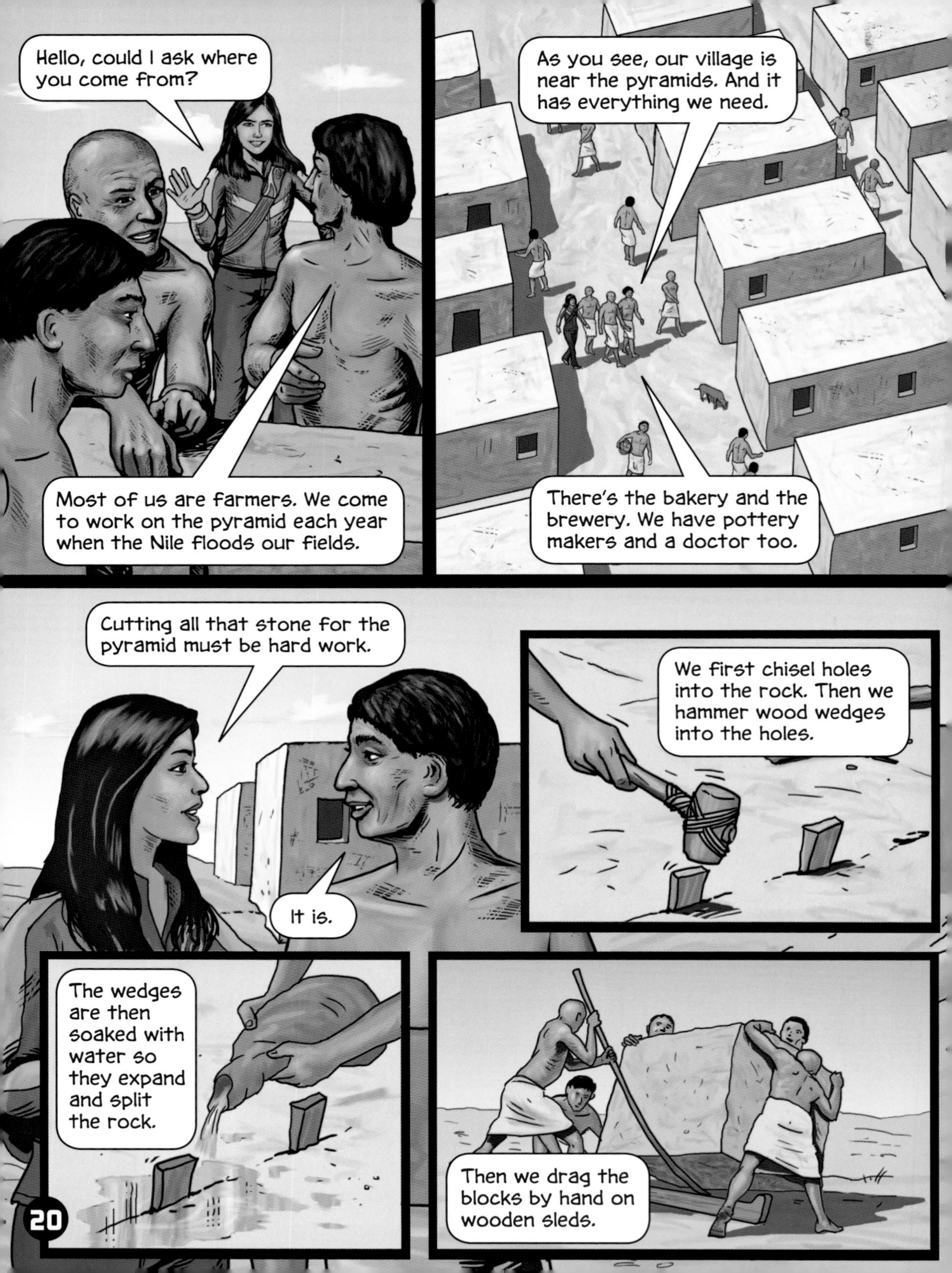
Hello, could I ask where you come from?
Most of us are farmers. We come to work on the pyramid each year when the Nile floods our fields.
As you see, our village is near the pyramids. And it has everything we need.
There's the bakery and the brewery. We have pottery makers and a doctor too.
Cutting all that stone for the pyramid must be hard work.
It is.
We first chisel holes into the rock. Then we hammer wood wedges into the holes.
The wedges are then soaked with water so they expand and split the rock.
Then we drag the blocks by hand on wooden sleds.

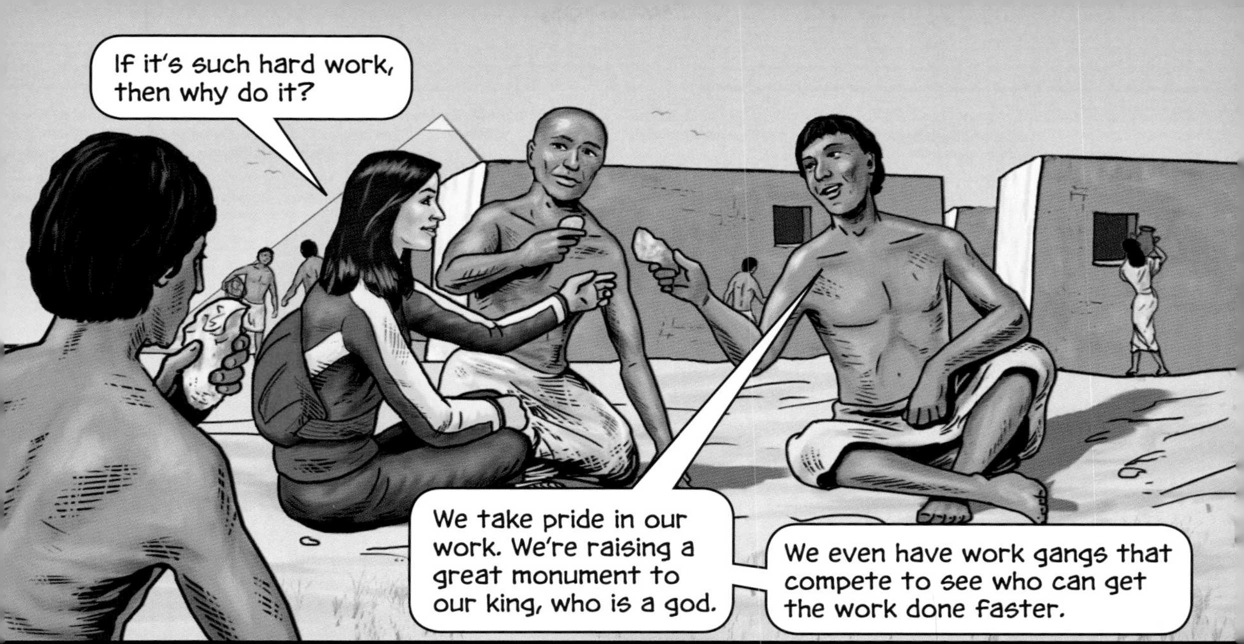
If it's such hard work, then why do it?
We take pride in our work. We're raising a great monument to our king, who is a god.
We even have work gangs that compete to see who can get the work done faster.

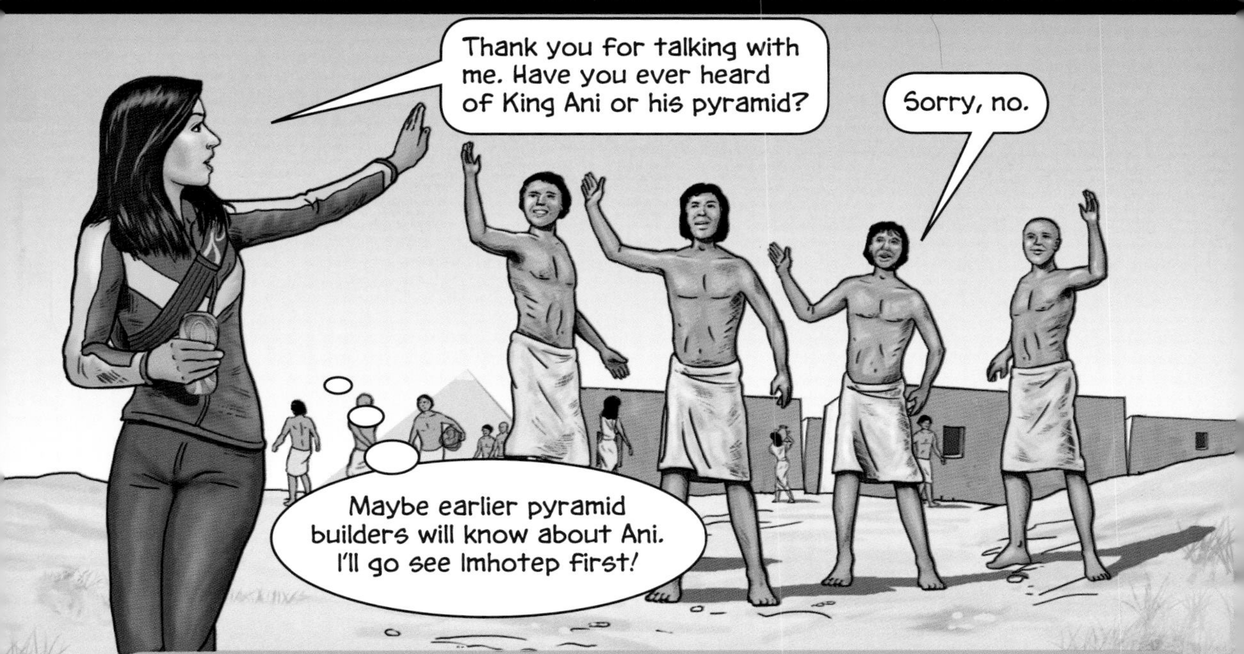
Thank you for talking with me. Have you ever heard of King Ani or his pyramid?
Sorry, no.
Maybe earlier pyramid builders will know about Ani. I'll go see Imhotep first!

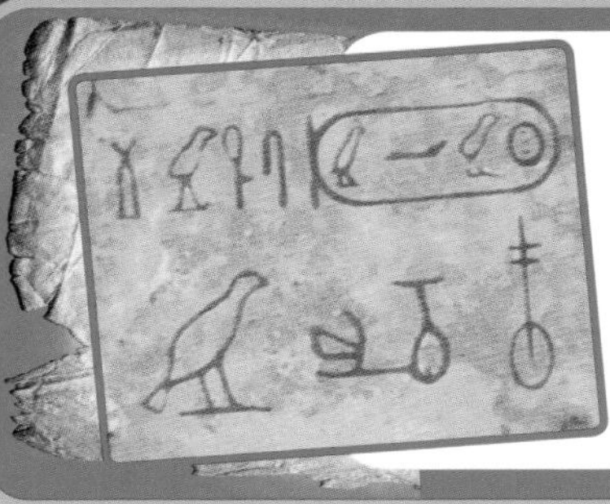

ANCIENT GRAFFITI

Archaeologists have found ancient graffiti on stones inside the Giza pyramids. The pyramid builders were split into work gangs. They had names like "Friends of Khufu" and "Drunkards of Menkaure." To show loyalty to the pharaoh, the workers scrawled their gang names into the stone blocks.

CHAPTER 4 THE FIRST PYRAMIDS

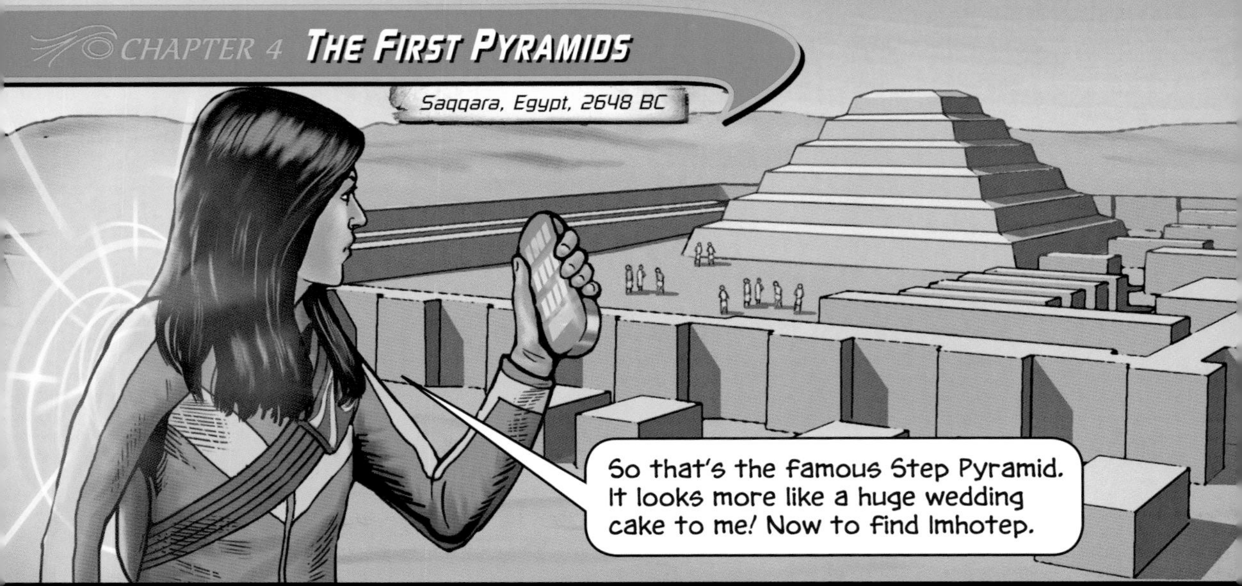
Saqqara, Egypt, 2648 BC
So that's the famous Step Pyramid. It looks more like a huge wedding cake to me! Now to find Imhotep.

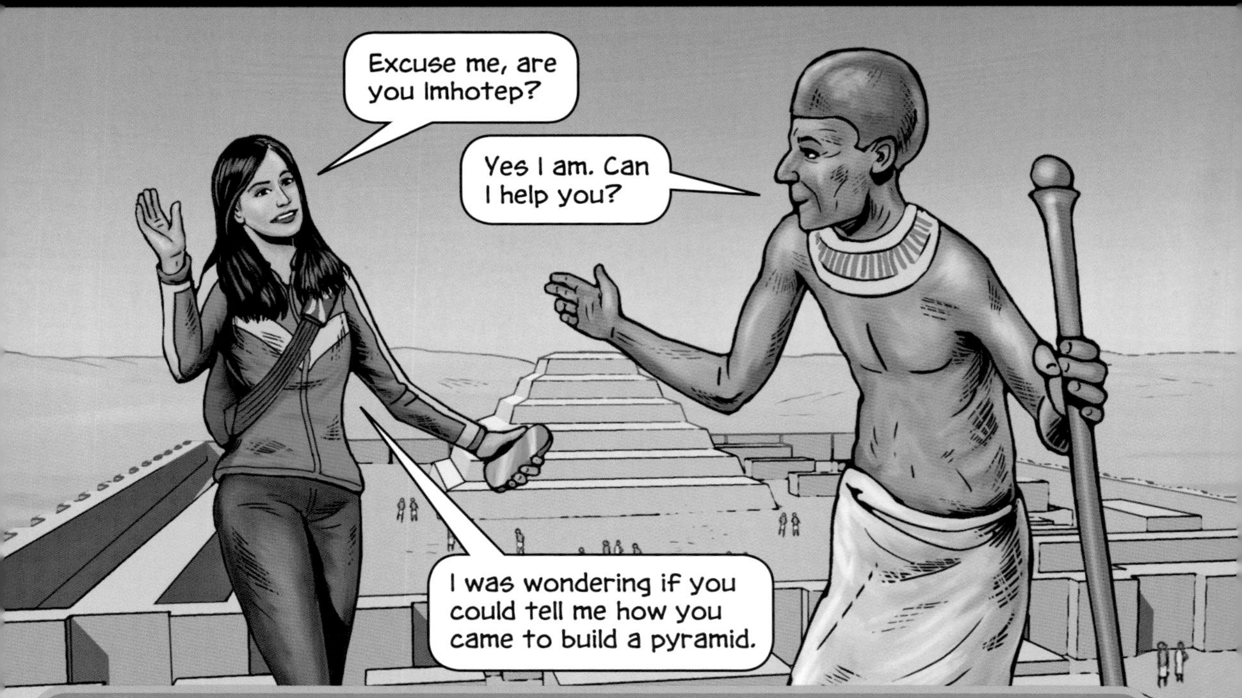
Excuse me, are you Imhotep?
Yes I am. Can I help you?
I was wondering if you could tell me how you came to build a pyramid.

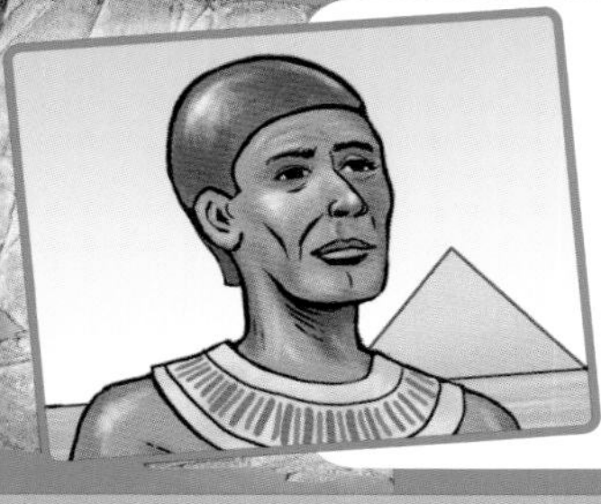

IMHOTEP

Imhotep was King Djoser's chancellor, high priest, and chief architect. Djoser's Step Pyramid is the world's oldest stone monument. Imhotep eventually became more famous than his king. Two thousand years after his death, Imhotep was worshipped as a god of wisdom.

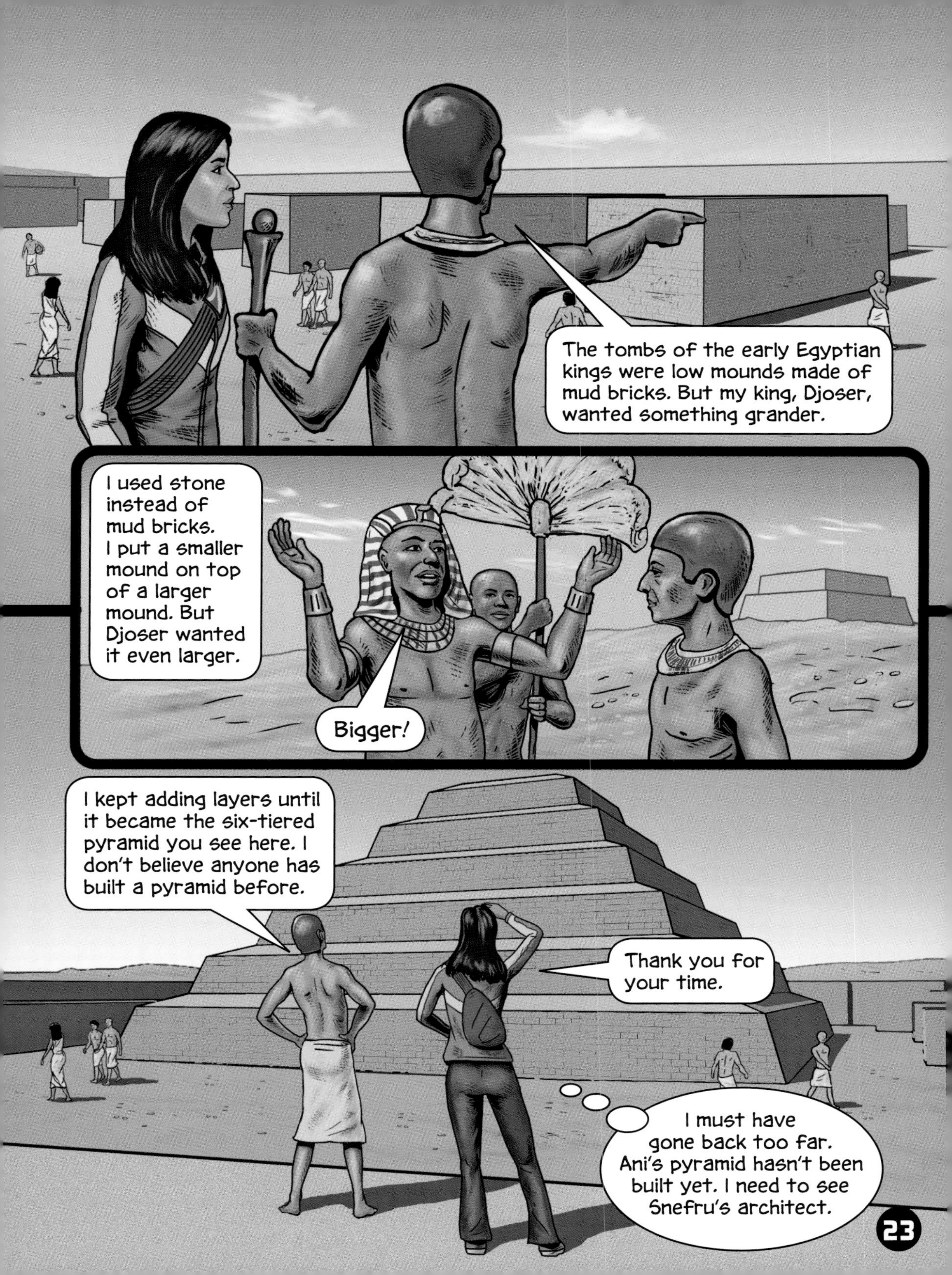

The tombs of the early Egyptian kings were low mounds made of mud bricks. But my king, Djoser, wanted something grander.
I used stone instead of mud bricks. I put a smaller mound on top of a larger mound. But Djoser wanted it even larger.
Bigger!
I kept adding layers until it became the six-tiered pyramid you see here. I don't believe anyone has built a pyramid before.
Thank you for your time.
I must have gone back too far. Ani's pyramid hasn't been built yet. I need to see Snefru's architect.

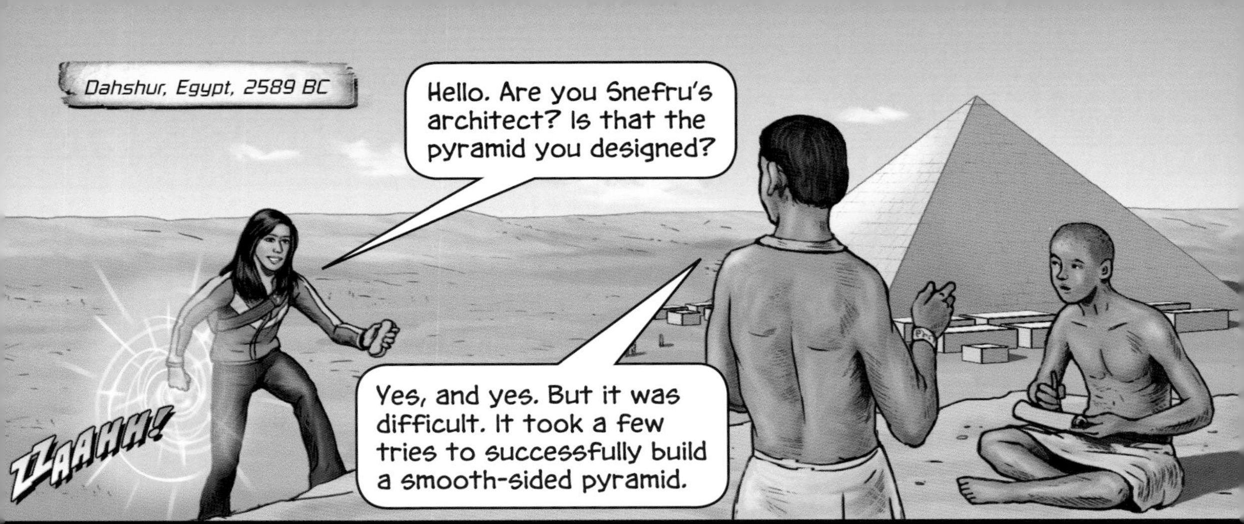

Dahshur, Egypt, 2589 BC
Hello. Are you Snefru's architect? Is that the pyramid you designed?
ZZAAHH!
Yes, and yes. But it was difficult. It took a few tries to successfully build a smooth-sided pyramid.

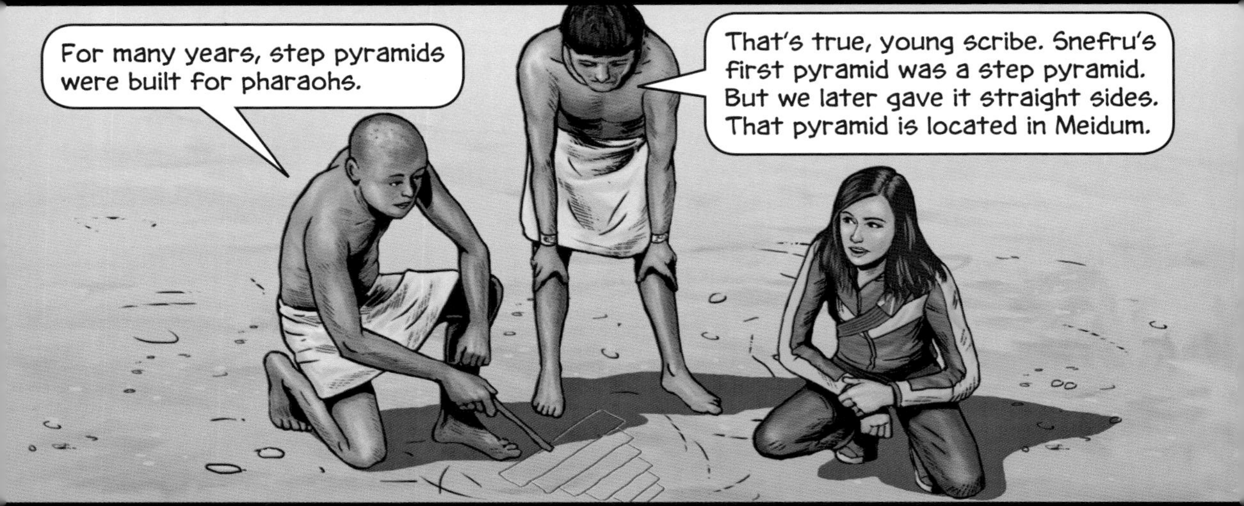

For many years, step pyramids were built for pharaohs.
That's true, young scribe. Snefru's first pyramid was a step pyramid. But we later gave it straight sides. That pyramid is located in Meidum.

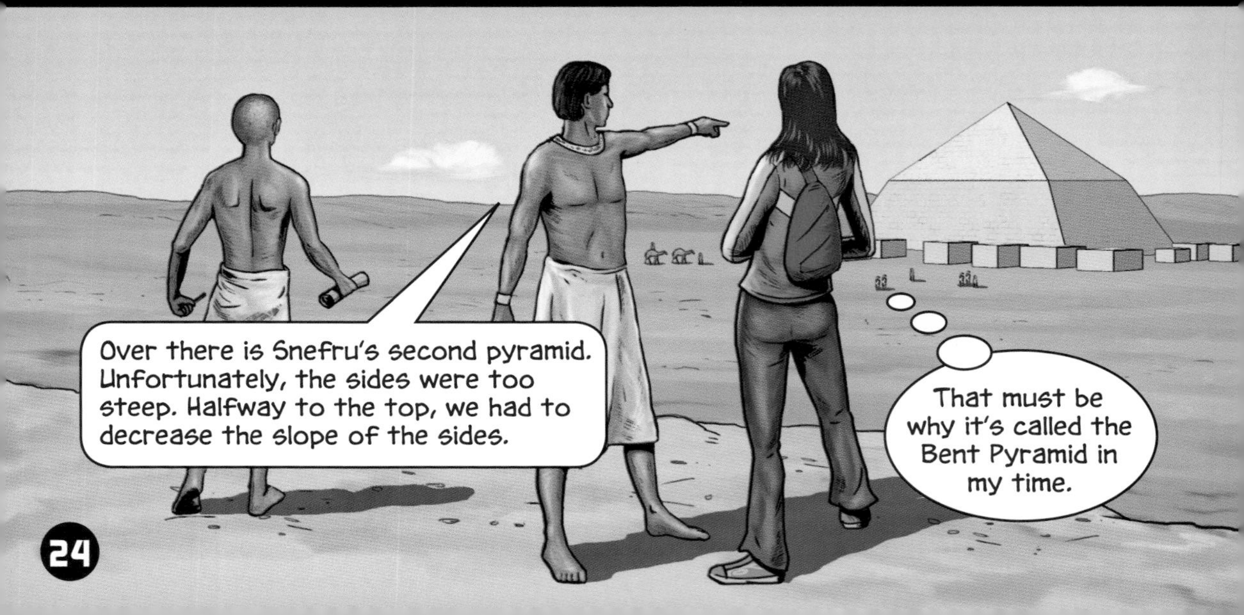

Over there is Snefru's second pyramid. Unfortunately, the sides were too steep. Halfway to the top, we had to decrease the slope of the sides.
That must be why it's called the Bent Pyramid in my time.

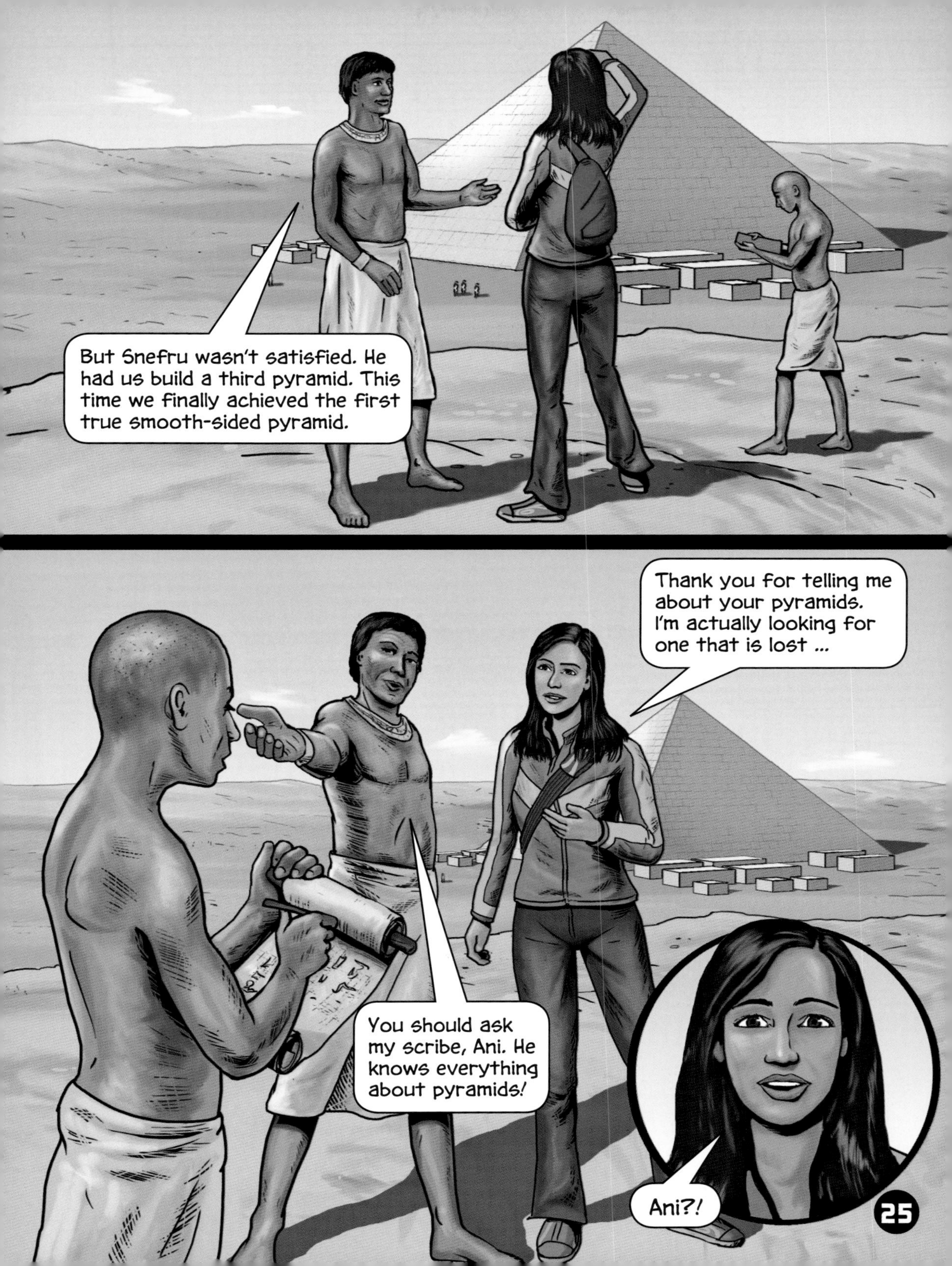
But Snefru wasn't satisfied. He had us build a third pyramid. This time we finally achieved the first true smooth-sided pyramid.
Thank you for telling me about your pyramids. I'm actually looking for one that is lost ...
You should ask my scribe, Ani. He knows everything about pyramids!
Ani?!

CHAPTER 5 THE TRUTH REVEALED

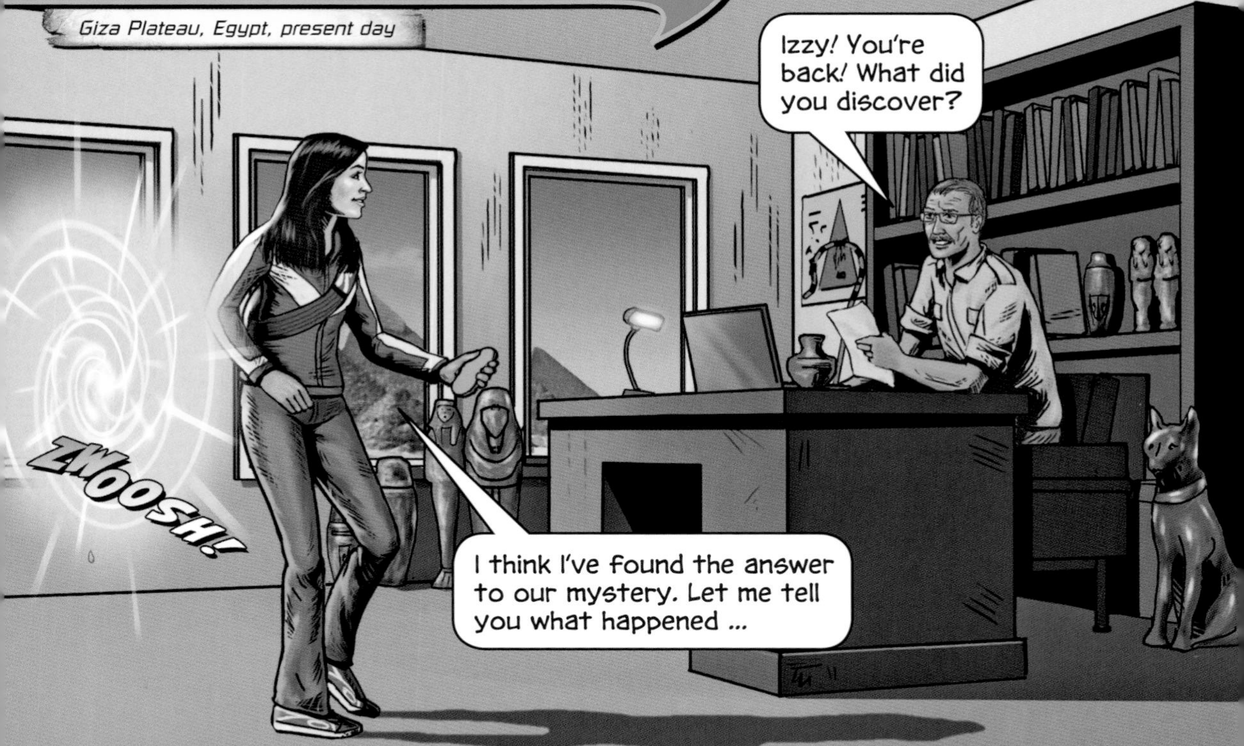
Giza Plateau, Egypt, present day
ZWOOSH!
Izzy! You're back! What did you discover?
I think I've found the answer to our mystery. Let me tell you what happened ...

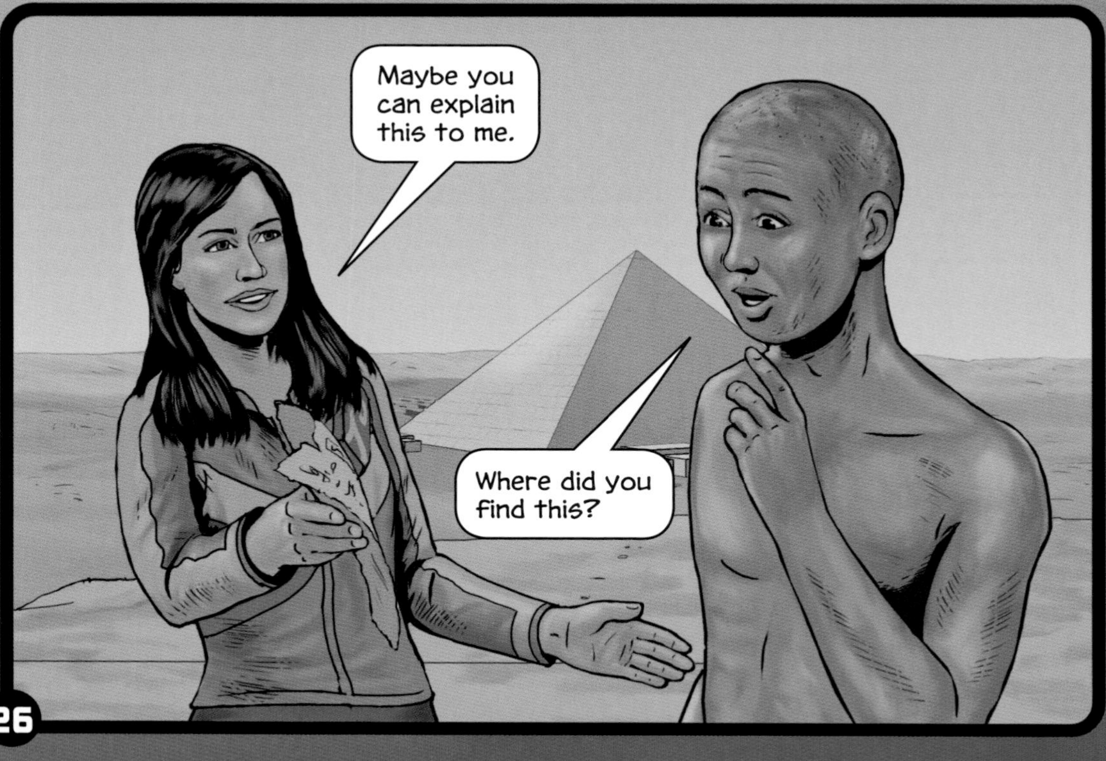
Maybe you can explain this to me.
Where did you find this?

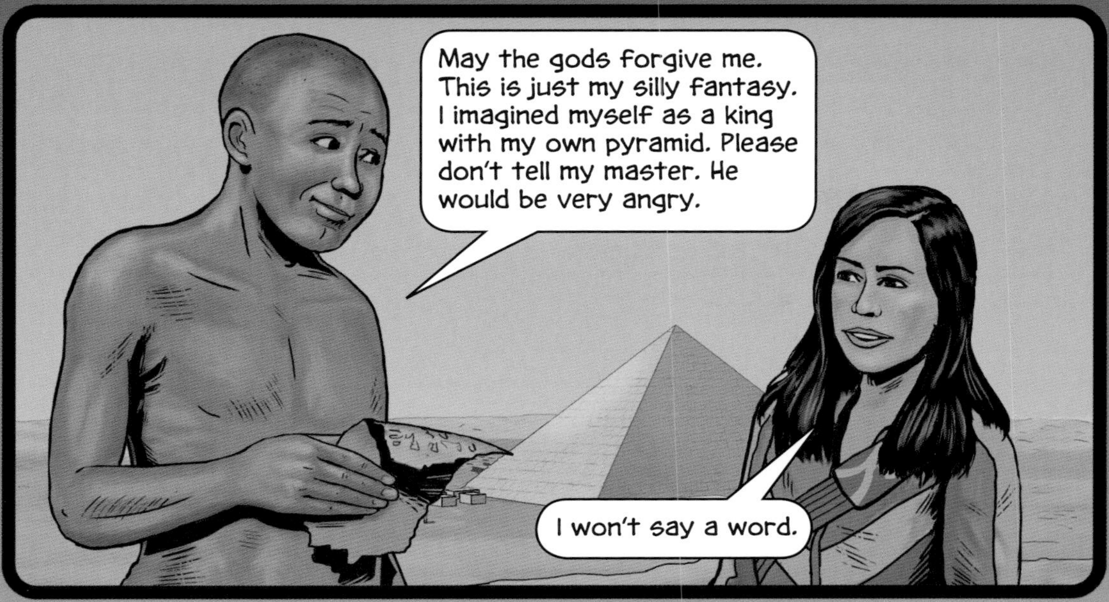
May the gods forgive me. This is just my silly fantasy. I imagined myself as a king with my own pyramid. Please don't tell my master. He would be very angry.
I won't say a word.

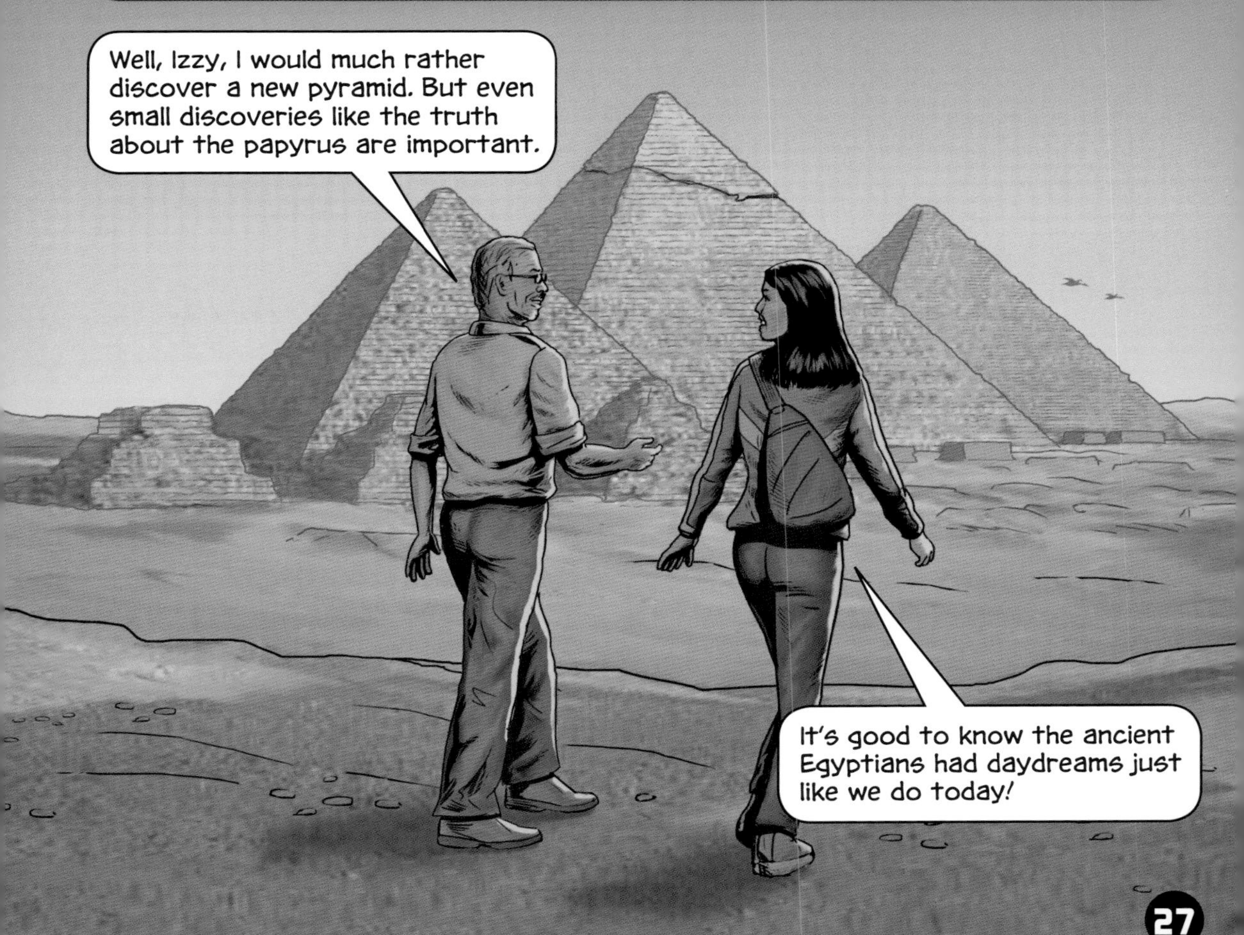
Well, Izzy, I would much rather discover a new pyramid. But even small discoveries like the truth about the papyrus are important.
It's good to know the ancient Egyptians had daydreams just like we do today!

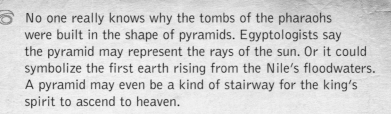

No one really knows why the tombs of the pharaohs were built in the shape of pyramids. Egyptologists say the pyramid may represent the rays of the sun. Or it could symbolize the first earth rising from the Nile's floodwaters. A pyramid may even be a kind of stairway for the king's spirit to ascend to heaven.

Iron was not yet used for tools when the pyramids were built. The pyramid builders used tools of wood, stone, and copper to create the immense monuments.

Tomb robbers have looted all the pyramids. There has never been an intact tomb found inside a pyramid. The Great Pyramid was robbed within 400 years of being built.

The Egyptians stopped building pyramids because of tomb robbers. About 3,500 years ago, pharaohs began to be buried in the Valley of the Kings. King Tut's tomb is found there.

Egyptologists believe it took about 20 years and 20,000 to 25,000 workers to build the Great Pyramid. There were about 4,000 primary workers, which included quarry workers, masons, and haulers. There were also about 16,000 to 20,000 secondary workers. These included ramp builders, tool makers, mortar mixers, and people who supplied food and clothing to all the other workers.

At one time, tourists were able to climb the Pyramids of Giza. But the practice was stopped because it was very dangerous, and it was damaging the pyramids. Today the pyramids face another problem—air pollution. The pyramids are very close to the large city of Cairo, Egypt. The pollution from all the traffic is causing the pyramids to erode more quickly.

The Great Pyramid was originally 480 feet (146 meters) tall and had smooth sides. But the high-quality stones that encased it were later removed for other structures and buildings. Today the Great Pyramid stands at about 450 feet (137 m) tall.

MORE ABOUT

Isabel Soto

NAME: Dr. Isabel "Izzy" Soto
DEGREES: History and Anthropology
BUILD: Athletic   **HAIR:** Dark Brown
EYES: Brown   **HEIGHT:** 5' 7"

W.I.S.P.: The Worldwide Inter-dimensional Space/Time Portal developed by Max Axiom at Axiom Laboratory.

BACKSTORY: Dr. Isabel "Izzy" Soto caught the history bug as a little girl. Every night, her grandfather told her about his adventures exploring ancient ruins in South America. He believed lost cultures teach people a great deal about history.

Izzy's love of cultures followed her to college. She studied history and anthropology. On a research trip to Thailand, she discovered an ancient stone with mysterious energy. Izzy took the stone to Super Scientist Max Axiom who determined that the stone's energy cuts across space and time. Harnessing the power of the stone, he built a device called the W.I.S.P. It opens windows to any place and any time. Izzy now travels through time to see history unfold before her eyes. Although she must not change history, she can observe and investigate historical events.

acre (AY-kur)—a measurement of area equal to 43,560 square feet (4,047 square meters); an acre is about the size of a football field

archaeologist (ar-kee-OL-uh-jist)—a scientist who studies how people lived in the past

architect (AR-ki-tekt)—a person who designs buildings and advises in their construction

artifact (AR-tuh-fakt)—an object used in the past that was made by people

graffiti (gruh-FEE-tee)—pictures drawn or words written on the walls of buildings or other surfaces

lubricate (LOO-bruh-kate)—to add a substance to allow the surfaces of two objects to easily slide over each other

monument (MON-yuh-muhnt)—a large structure built to honor a person or an event

mummify (MUH-mih-fy)—to preserve a body with special salts and cloth to make it last for a very long time

papyrus (puh-PYE-ruhss)—a tall water plant that grows in northern Africa and southern Europe; a material that is written on can be made from the stems of this plant

pharaoh (FAIR-oh)—a king of ancient Egypt

plateau (pla-TOH)—an area of high, flat land

quarry (KWOR-ee)—a place where stone is dug out of the ground

rite (RAYHT)—an action performed as part of a religious ceremony

tomb (TOOM)—a grave, room, or building that holds a dead body

READ MORE

Adamson, Heather. *Ancient Egypt: An Interactive History Adventure.* You Choose Books. Mankato, Minn.: Capstone Press, 2010.

Forest, Christopher. *Pyramids of Ancient Egypt.* Ancient Egyptian Civilization. Mankato, Minn.: Capstone Press, 2012.

MacDonald, Fiona. *Solving the Mysteries of the Pyramids.* Digging Into History. New York: Marshall Cavendish Benchmark, 2009.

Putnam, James. *Pyramid.* DK Eyewitness Books. New York: DK Pub., 2011.

Williams, Brenda and Brian. *Reach for the Stars: Ancient Egyptian Pyramids.* Fusion. Chicago: Raintree, 2008.

INTERNET SITES

FactHound offers a safe, fun way to find Internet sites related to this book. All sites on FactHound have been researched by our staff.

Here's all you do:

Visit *www.facthound.com*

Type in this code: 9781429675444

Check out projects, games and lots more at
www.capstonekids.com

INDEX